FLOELLA BENJAMIN, writer, t
caster, was born in Trinida
worked in all aspects of broa
is for children's television
many years. She has writter
is dedicated to all children
need a guiding hand.

She is married and has two children, Aston and Alvina.

elevision producer and broad-
one of six children. She has
adcasting, but her greatest love
occasion which she has worked for
written several books, and this latest
especially those who might

For Goodness Sake!

A guide to choosing right from wrong

Floella Benjamin

Illustrated by Peter Doherty

HarperCollins*Publishers*

HarperCollins*Publishers*
77–85 Fulham Palace Road, London W6 8JB

First published in Great Britain
in 1994 by HarperCollins*Publishers*

1 3 5 7 9 10 8 6 4 2

A catalogue record for this book is
available from the British Library

0551 02799-1

Printed and bound in Great Britain by
HarperCollinsManufacturing Glasgow

Contents

Acknowledgements

I would like to thank:

Stephen Williams and the pupils of Kingsdale School, Dulwich.

The pupils of St John's C.E. Middle School, Stanmore.

Maurice Lynch, Director of the BFSS National Religious Education Centre.

Barry Allcott and Ray Bruce, of CTVC.

My dear friend Nicola Cope, who even though she suffers greatly with spina bifida, is always ready and willing to help and care for others.

Pat and Robert McLean for all their help and advice.

My parents for doing everything to give me and my brothers and sisters, wisdom, common sense and confidence.

Finally a big thank you to Keith, Aston and Alvina for all their help and patience.

Chapter 1

Introduction

WHEN I WAS A LITTLE GIRL I religiously went to Sunday school with my five brothers and sisters. I used to look forward to going because it was great fun. It was very exciting being together with lots of other children all dressed in our Sunday best clothes, which weren't expensive or fashionable but were always clean, crisp, freshly starched and ironed. It always gave us a sense of pride in how we looked.

At Sunday school we learnt about creation, about the wonders of the world and how to love and care for others. We were encouraged to understand that many of the things which happened to us in our lives were very similar to what happened to people centuries ago. It's amazing but many of the situations in the Bible are just as relevant today as they were then. The circumstances may have been different then but the outcome was the same. Perhaps history repeats itself because we have to learn the same lessons over and over again every generation. Noah's Ark is a great example of how things got so bad they had to make a fresh start and some were given the chance to start again. You may not want to believe in the Bible but in order to make up your mind, you must first of all read and understand what it's all about. I have a saying which goes, "In order to break the rules, you must first know what the rules are" and, as I see it, the Bible is basically a set of rules for life.

Pig style

You might not get a chance to go to Sunday school and learn about right and wrong, good and evil but even so you can take the opportunity to learn during school assembly or religious studies. It's really worth opening your mind and taking it all in as it will form a foundation for life and help you decide what is morally right. We all need a solid foundation to build our lives on so that when we hit difficult patches we have the strength and armour to deal with them.

I always think of life as being like the well known nursery story of *The Three Little Pigs* which I'm sure you know. But have you ever thought about what it's teaching us. In the story one pig builds a house of straw, one a house of wood and the third a house of stone. The big bad wolf comes along and blows down the house of straw and the house of wood but not the house of stone. This story has a much deeper meaning than you first imagine. What it's saying is that the wolf represents all the challenges and bad things in life and is always there lurking and waiting to get you. If you build your life without strong found-ations, he will easily blow you down. The slightest crisis will cause you to become vulnerable. But if you prepare your life in a solid way and build it with bricks of love, honesty, compassion, faith and strength of mind, you will be strong enough to face any challenge.

To help you face these challenges you must practise what I call the three "Cs". They are "**consideration**", which means thinking of others, "**contentment**", that's being happy with what you've got and not being consumed by greed and envy, and "**confidence**", that's believing in yourself and loving yourself which makes it easy for you to love others. Practise these and you'll get a clear feeling and understanding of how to live and get the most out of your life. It can be an exciting, rewarding and satisfying path to be on if you style yourself on the third little pig!

Agony and ecstasy

Your body has its own natural source of ecstasy which you can trigger off at will. There is no need for you to take any drugs to get a high. By doing good, being happy with yourself and what you have, you can get that feeling of ecstasy and get a buzz out of living every day to the full. The secret is to find simple but exciting things that make you feel happy. I'm not talking about materialistic things, with those you'll find the more you have the more you want. The latest gadget always looks more attractive than the last and you end up reaching out for the newest one, so you'll never be happy for very long. Things don't have to cost the earth to make you happy. Simple things which we take for granted can bring far more happiness, put a smile on your face and show everybody you're a happy and contented person who is not being consumed by envy, greed and evil.

Perhaps the circumstances in your life are not easy for you to bear and make it hard for you to feel good and happy with yourself. You may be feeling abused, unloved and tormented. But what you mustn't do is allow the evil of others to turn you into a bad person. You have to be strong and pray that your situation will change for the better. It will if you talk to someone you can trust about it. Life cannot be one long torture forever. Don't run away from it because what you might run into could be an even worse nightmare. You could find yourself in a situation a hundred times worse than you ever imagined. If life is totally unbearable, then there are people, places and organizations that you can go to for help. They will try to make your life happier, make you feel more worthwhile and end the agony in your life.

Read on

I hope when you read this book you will learn that doing good makes you feel good. The more you choose to do the right thing the easier it becomes.

So read on …

Chapter 2

Good and Evil: Knowing the difference

THIS BOOK IS ABOUT GOOD AND EVIL, which to put it more simply is about understanding and knowing the difference between right and wrong. A young girl I know recently asked me if there was such a thing as "the devil". She had seen something on television that had scared her, you know the sort of thing, a man holding a fork, dressed up with horns and a tail.

I thought for a moment and said to her, "Yes, but there is also a God and they both want to live inside you." You see, all human beings are capable of doing good or evil and there is always a battle going on between those two forces to try and get the upper hand. It's a battle that rages all the time in everything we do, like the moment when you are about to steal something. The voice in your head says, "Are you sure I should do this? ... Yea, go on, think of the thrill and excitement." For some reason, evil or bad things always show themselves as more exciting, more glamorous, more thrilling and daring. But if you just have the strength to hang on to your good side and think of the consequences, the long-term outcome will be so much better and you will feel so good about yourself. It's something that has to be practised. The more you are aware and conscious of the battle, the easier it will become for good to conquer. No one really wants to be bad to their fellow man and even if they are, they confess their sins at sometime. They always end up saying sorry. You always regret doing bad things but you never regret doing good things.

What's right and what's wrong

What a lot of young people don't understand is how to

decide what is right and what is wrong. Well it's quite simple, something that is wrong is doing something that affects others or yourself in a bad way, from throwing a piece of litter on the floor to mugging someone, from taking drugs to playing truant. Good is when you and others are made to feel confident, secure and happy as a result of your actions.

Everyone has a voice in their head, they hold conversations with it and they follow its instructions. Some people imagine a face or even a person. We call it our conscience and like every other part of our mind and body it has to be developed and trained so that it works efficiently. We have to learn to know the difference between right and wrong. So who chooses what is right and wrong? ... Well you do! The question you should ask yourself is "what effect will my actions have on others?" In other words "what will be the consequences of my actions?" You may not realize it, but everything you do, even the simplest of things, has an effect on those around you, in either a negative or a positive way. Like throwing a pebble in a pond the ripples spread and expand to touch every part of the pond. If you look at the pond as your life and all your actions are the pebbles, you will start to see and understand what I mean.

Many of you may find it difficult to imagine that your actions can affect people like that. The reason is that you have a very low opinion of yourself, low self-esteem. "Oh, no I haven't", I hear some of you say. I'm not talking about brazen cockiness – that is having a false opinion of yourself. I'm talking about real deep inside confidence, the belief that you are a worthwhile and valuable person with something to offer society no matter how young you are. When you truly believe that about yourself you are untouchable, no one can defeat you, no matter what they say or do. Believe it, you are very important. We are all important and all our actions are intertwined and they affect everyone around us.

Chain reaction

Let's imagine an incident that shows how a foolish action can have this ripple effect and hurt dozens of people. This is an imaginary story but events like it are happening in real life every day.

It was Monday morning and Wayne and Nick had bunked off school again. As they turned the corner near Nick's house they both spotted the car at the same time. It was parked outside the old people's flats. It looked only a few months old and its GTI radiator badge sparkled in the sun.

The car's owner was a young lady doctor called Claire Ubegwi, she had worked and saved hard to buy it and this was the first day she had used it. She was out visiting a sick patient who was too ill to leave her flat on the top floor.

Wayne had seen his older brother get into and start cars loads of times and within thirty seconds he was inside and had the engine started. "Hey, have you ever driven a car before?" asked Nick as Wayne crunched the gears and spun the wheels in a cloud of burning rubber. "Na, but I've seen my brother do it, it's easy."

Inside the flats Claire was examining old Mrs Ryan. The old lady was in a bad way, her breathing was shallow and every few minutes she had a coughing fit. Claire could see that her condition was becoming more and more serious and it looked as if she was going to need an ambulance quickly.

"This'll do a hundred and twenty!" shouted Wayne over the sound of the blasting stereo. "There's a bit of dual carriageway up ahead; we'll see what we can get it up to."

P.C. Dodds was just starting his shift in his panda car when he spotted the GTI speeding in the opposite direction, he could tell immediately that it was being driven by someone young and inexperienced. He radioed in the number and quickly turned round to give chase.

Back at the flats Dr Ubegwi was frantically pleading with the ambulance controller. "But she needs an ambulance now, not in forty-five minutes!" Old Mrs Ryan started another coughing fit, "Oh never mind," snapped Claire looking at her patient anxiously, "I'll take her myself!" It was a long struggle but Claire managed to get the old lady into the lift and down to street level.

Supporting her with one hand Claire fumbled in her bag for her car keys. Then she looked up and down the street in disbelief … her car had gone!

P.C. Dodds was closing in fast on the GTI, he could see now that it was being driven by a young boy no more than twelve years old. He glanced at the speedo, they were doing seventy miles an hour in a built-up area! He knew there was a short piece of dual carriageway coming up but he also knew there was a school at the end of it. The procedure was to back off and keep the car in sight until other police units could join the chase, but just then the driver of the GTI spotted him and accelerated hard, swerving madly across the road. P.C. Dodds had to work hard just to keep up as they joined the dual carriageway.

Mrs Hamley was tired, she had just taken her class to the museum and was herding them off the coach. "Line up against the wall and stop messing around!" she bellowed at the laughing school kids. In that instant she heard the screech of tyres, a red blur came from behind the coach and slammed into the wall scattering the kids like nine-pins.

Meanwhile back at the flats Claire took off her coat and covered the now still body of Mrs Ryan. She had tried the kiss of life for ten minutes but it was hopeless, Mrs Ryan was dead.

P.C. Dodds arrived on the scene seconds after the accident. The driver of the GTI had gone through the windscreen, he hadn't even been wearing his seatbelt. He was still alive, just. The passenger wasn't so lucky. Neither was one of the school children, she had taken the full force of the crash. Everywhere there were children and adults in various states of shock and injury. It was the worst accident P.C. Dodds had ever seen. Six months later he was forced to leave the police force suffering from stress and mental prolems.

Moral
If Wayne and Nick hadn't foolishly taken the car for fun, many people's lives wouldn't have been affected. If they had done the right thing by not stealing it the consequences would have been so different. They stole, ignored, abused, injured and killed, all at other people's expense.

1. Make a list of how many people were affected by Wayne and Nick's stupid act.

2. Try to imagine how far the ripples spread.

Giving and receiving

A well-known saying from the Bible is "Whatsoever a man soweth, that he shall also reap." This means that whatever someone sends out in word or deed will return to them; what you give you will receive back. Give hate and you will receive hate. Give love and you will receive love, give criticism and you will receive criticism, tell lies and you will be lied to, cheat and you will be cheated.

Think about it. If you show hatred to someone in your class, what happens? They will probably hate you back. If you show them friendship then they will more than likely show you friendship. So it's worthwhile behaving towards people the way you'd like them to behave towards you. I know some of you might say, "Good, I want to be hated!" Come on admit it, deep down do you really want to be hated? You get a much better feeling when you are liked and you know it.

Why do people do bad things?

There are many reasons why people do bad things. Many youngsters feel unloved and unwanted, they think no one cares about them so they lash out and hurt others. Some live with unemployment and poverty, but are surrounded by glitzy advertising and shops full of goodies. Naturally they feel jealous or envious of what others have. They want expensive, exciting belongings too, but they have no means of getting them honestly, which is why so many turn to crime.

Young people are surrounded by despair and hopelessness. Everywhere there is death, starvation, crime, war and injustice. People in charge appear to be out of step with the real world and their actions sometimes seem to make things worse rather than better. Young people often feel let down by society, so as a means of escape many turn to drugs and crime.

These are a few of the main reasons why people do bad things. No one is born bad, but the surroundings we live in can make otherwise honest and caring people go off the rails.

It's not my problem … is it?

We all want to be happy and safe, we want a world where we can grow up without fear and yet the world in which we live seems to be plunging towards its destruction, and we seem incapable of saving it. I've heard many people say, "Why bother trying to save it? – it's not worth saving anyway!" But hang on a minute, what kind of talk is this? We can make things better, it's not a problem, the solution is quite simple. The answer lies within us all, every one of us. The answer is not doing bad things – if everyone, every single person on the planet did what was morally right, the world would change overnight. If no one stole, no one hated, no one killed or hurt others, if everyone considered each other and cared about all human beings as they care about themselves, then we would see a change! If we thought about things we have done in the past and tried to put them right, we would be well on the way to a better world. If we try to help those who need help, instead of just helping ourselves, things would get better.

So you see it is your problem, you as an individual have to make an effort to change things, and slowly but surely you will start to change things for the better.

It will be back to haunt you

It's amazingly difficult for young people to imagine themselves as an adult, a parent or especially as an old age
pensioner. I don't know why this is , I suppose it's because
it's very difficult to imagine something which you have
absolutely no experience of, it's like asking someone to
imagine what it's like to walk on the moon. Nevertheless I
still want you to try to imagine yourself ten or twenty years
from now. Some of you may be parents with young children, you may have saved hard and bought a car, or even
your own home. You will be just like the thousands of
people you see all around you at the supermarket doing
their shopping or taking their children for a walk in the
park. And you will feel just how they feel when your car is
stolen or your house is burgled or your child is hurt or
threatened.

Now try very, very hard to imagine what it would feel
like to be an old age pensioner, afraid to go out because of
the fear of being attacked and robbed. Put yourself in their
position. The amazing thing is that you will be responsible
for the way things are twenty or thirty years from now.
What you do now will return to haunt you later in life. If
you behave in a socially and morally bad way, then you
will find the things you do now will be done to you.
Imagine beating up an eighty-year-old lady for a few coins.
Think about how she feels, and say to yourself, "That
could be me one day, how would I feel?"

Daily challenge

Here is a really good saying which I love to think about
when I get up each day, "Today is the first day of the rest

of my life," in other words no matter what has gone before, each new day brings a new challenge and a chance to make a new beginning. If you think like that then every day becomes an exciting opportunity to do good. Saying things to yourself is a good way of reminding yourself of your aims and goals. Another good way of remembering what you have to do is to write it down, write yourself a letter, laying out your thoughts on paper so that you can read them and remember them.

Here are a few challenging but common sense ideas as a guide on how to behave. You can remember them or write them down and carry them with you.

Love yourself and love one another.

Do not hurt or bully others.

Do not take drugs or abuse your body.

Do not lie or cheat.

Do not destroy your surroundings or your planet.

Do not damage property or things.

Do not crave for other people's possessions.

Do not talk badly about others.

Do not wish bad things to happen to others.

Do not steal.

It's a tough list but if you can practise some of these challenges the consequences of your actions will be good, not bad. It takes a big effort but you can do it.

Chapter 3

He's not heavy, he's my brother

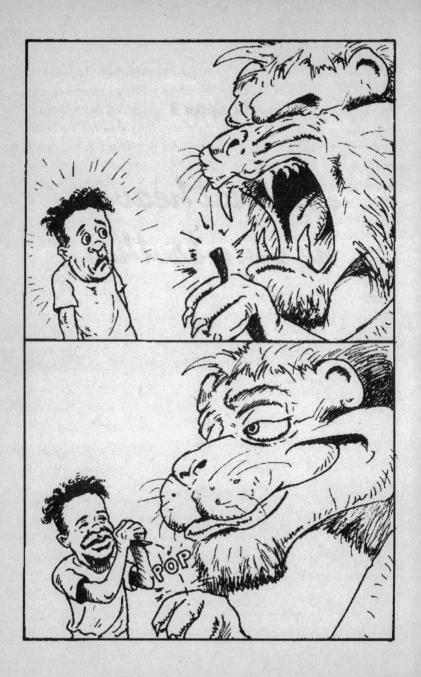

SOMETIMES IT'S DIFFICULT to remember that every single person on this earth has feelings just like you and I. When you look around it seems that everyone is happy and secure and having fun and you're the only person with problems. Well it's just not true. When you read about famous or rich people in the newspaper it's hard to imagine them having worries and anxieties and yet often they have worse problems than any of us. One thing I've learnt is that if you care for others someone will care for you. If you are selfish and uncaring then no one will care what happens to you. It mustn't be a way of getting people to like you, it must be a true and genuine feeling from the heart. People can tell if your attempts to be caring are false. Then they will dislike you even more. Caring for each other every day of our lives is important, even in small ways.

It's not good enough doing one big thing for charity for example then going round for the rest of the year in a selfish little world of your own. Caring for others means putting yourself in other people's situations and then doing your best to help them.

Feelings

A very interesting game to play is to look at someone, someone who is quite different from you, for example, a blind person or someone in a wheelchair and really try to imagine what they feel like, put yourself in their place.

What you have to do is think about your feelings and problems less, put yourself in other people's situation and imagine what it must be like to have their problems. The amazing thing is there is nearly always someone worse off than you.

I sometimes visit hospitals for very sick children. When I'm there I realize any petty little problems I have are tiny compared to what those children and their families have to go through. People can be so brave it amazes me. When I leave it makes me realize that I am a very lucky person indeed and it makes me want to help others more and more.

Old folks

Nowadays people seem to have lost all respect for old folks. Old people are treated with scorn and made to feel isolated, unwanted and unimportant. Fortunately though, there are some cultures who value their old folks for their wisdom and experience. In their homes you'll find granny and grandad living alongside toddlers and teenagers making the most of the extended family by caring for each other. For some children this is the first step towards learning how to care for and respect old folks.

Even if you haven't got grandparents nearby, look around your neighbourhood and see who might be old and frail. Imagine what it must be like for them. Imagine what you will feel like when you are old. Just going to the shops when you're old can be a frightening and hazardous undertaking. Old people nowadays are terrified of young people, they associate them with being mugged, or being beaten up, that's why they might be bad-tempered or defensive. Try to find a way to show them that you care. A simple thing like opening a door or stepping aside for them to get past or giving up your seat on a bus will show that you respect and care for them. Talking to old people can be quite an eye-opener, they have so much experience and can pass it on to you if only you'll listen. They may seem frail and slow now but they were once just like you, strong and fit and energetic!

Help yourself by helping others

The feeling you get when you help someone is so good that it sometimes can give you goose pimples. It can make your heart swell up and make you feel so happy. It certainly beats kicking sand in someone's face. By helping and caring for others you help yourself to feel good. Others may say you are a goody-goody, but don't let them stop you, be strong, hold up your head and remember it feels good when you help others. Of course helping others can be good for you as well. You never know one day you might need help too and as I've said before, "You reap what you sow."

A thorny problem

A long time ago in Roman times there lived a boy called Androcles. He was a poor boy whose parents had died. He had to fend for himself and as he had no home he found a cave to live in far from the town.

One day as he sat alone in his cave a huge lion walked in. Naturally Androcles was terrified, he shook with fear in a dark corner of the cave as the lion stretched out across the cave blocking any chance of escape. But as Androcles watched the lion he realized that the poor animal was in great pain. Its paw was swollen and bleeding where a sharp thorn was deeply embedded in it. Plucking up all his courage Androcles slowly edged forward out of the shadows towards the lion. Ever so gently he took the lion's paw, pulled out the thorn, washed the wound and bandaged it.

Gradually as the days passed the lion's paw healed and he and Androcles became friends. Androcles and the lion shared the cave for many months until one day some Roman soldiers captured Androcles and took him to Rome to be sold as a slave.

But Androcles hated being a slave and refused to work. So he was sentenced to be fed to the lions at the Coliseum. Androcles was thrown into the arena in front of the Emperor and a huge crowd of Romans. A gate swung open and out rushed a ferocious lion straight at Androcles. But just before it leapt on him it skidded to a halt, instead of tearing him to pieces it rolled over on its back purring loudly. Then Androcles realized it was his friend, the lion who had also been captured and brought to Rome. The Emperor and the crowd were amazed, they stood up and cheered as Androcles walked around the arena with the lion at his side. Then the Emperor ordered Androcles and the lion to be set free and given a home to live in.

Moral

This is a wonderful story, it has several messages from which we can learn. Androcles felt sorry for the lion but it took great courage to emerge from the shadows and take the lion's paw in his hand.

Sometimes we need to have great courage to do something which is really frightening. Our first attempt at caring for others may be like that, taking the hand of someone who needs help can be a little bit scary – you're never sure whether or not they might tell you to get lost!

Of course the main message is that reaching out and caring for someone can have its rewards in the long term. If you show kindness and love to others then one day it will be returned to you in the most unexpected way.

Some ways to start caring

When you care about others it doesn't mean you're a creep or a crawler, it means that you are taking others into consideration. You may feel a little worried about helping others or may not know where to start. If this is the case then the first thing you must do is put yourself in the position of someone who needs help or needs to be shown that someone cares.

1. Someone at school may be lonely or being bullied. This is your chance to go in and help them, show them that they're not alone.

2. Be kind and say something nice to someone, like "thank you". Those two words can mean so much and can show that you really care.

3. When you cross the road on a zebra crossing and someone makes an effort to stop for you, wave and smile a thank you.

4. Find out if there are any groups in your area that help old folks or disabled people.

5. Give away any old toys or old clothes you don't need any more to a jumble sale or a charity shop.

6. They say charity begins at home, help out with the chores.

7. If you know someone who is ill, send them a card saying "get well soon".

8. Send thank you letters to people who give you presents or invite you to their parties or take you out on a treat.

9. Consider others when you are out playing, people nearby may be ill or have small babies sleeping. If they ask you to keep the noise down don't be rude and abusive.

10. Graffiti and damage to property can cause a great deal of distress, don't spoil other people's property or surroundings.

These are some of the first steps on the way to becoming a caring person. Try it, you could grow to like it. Remember, one day you might need someone to care for you.

Dear Floella,

One day on a holiday my cousin and I were playing football with some boys. I was in mid-field and my cousin was in goal. Half way into the game my cousin kicked the ball and suddenly his shoe came off because his shoe wasn't tied up properly. When he went to get his shoe he stepped on glass and cut his foot.

It was a nasty cut so I picked him up and took him to the clinic, it was right near his house.

Ahmed Deria

Dear Floella,
When I was in primary school I was playing
football. There was a boy who wasn't very
good at football. Half way through the
game someone took a powerful shot at
goal and the boy who wasn't very good
at football got in the way of the ball and
it came off him and went over the goal-
keepers head and in. Then everyone started
shouting at him and calling him names but
not me and my friend, we told them to
leave him alone and they did.

John O'Neill

Dear Floella,
My little brother's favourite toy was his
bicycle because he could ride it in the park
with his friends. One day he left it in the
park and went to buy ice cream. When he
came back into the park, the bicycle was not
there. He called me and we looked everywhere but it was gone. He started to cry and
whenever he saw his friends riding their
bikes he cried more and more.

I had been saving money to buy a
computer game and I took this money
which was sixty pounds and I bought him
a new bike. He was happy and I was happy
and that shows that I care more for my
brother than for myself.

Mohamed Musa

Chapter 4

The love of money is the root of all evil

IF YOU ASK ANYONE what they would like more than anything else, ninety-nine per cent of them would say they want to be rich, to have loads and loads of money. In fact most of the young people asked said they wanted to be rich *and* famous, in that order!

Money is nowadays the single most important thing in people's lives. I think this is a sad state to get into. Sure, having money is nice and it allows you to have the things you want. But the problem with money is that it brings out the worst in people who crave it. There is nothing wrong with money, after all as the song says "Money makes the world go round". The problem arises when people allow money to corrupt them, when they allow all other feelings and considerations to be controlled by their desire for money. In other words they are prepared to sell their souls for it. Hence the saying "The love of money is the root of all evil".

The society we live in has made money into a god. Advertisers try hard to make us want more and more by making things look incredibly glamorous and making us think we desire things we don't really want or need. Children are made to feel like outcasts unless they have the right brand of trainers or the latest computer. It's very difficult to break away from the need for material things and many young people who cannot afford expensive clothes and trainers become so desperate to get them, they turn to crime. They either steal the things they want or they steal the money to buy them.

Some people like to have lots of money because it gives them power over others. Money makes them feel important because people look up to those who have money, but really money has no power at all.

One of the oldest sayings is "Money isn't everything", and it's so true. No one can live without it in the modern world, but if it makes us unhappy and causes us to do evil things to each other then we should ask ourselves, is it really worth it? It's far better to be poor and happy than rich and evil. You can be rich in love and happiness and contentment which are worth far more than materialistic things.

Many wealthy people are never sure whether people like them for themselves or for their money. Sometimes they even hide the fact that they have money because they are afraid people will try to take advantage of them. So you see money doesn't always bring happiness.

You can't take it with you

Jesus often spoke to his followers about money and the evils it brings. Once he told them, "Beware! Be on your guard against greed of every kind, for even when a man has more than enough, his wealth does not give him life." There was a rich man whose land produced plenty of crops, so much in fact that he had nowhere to store the produce. So he decided to pull down his warehouses and build bigger ones so that he could store more food. He felt very pleased with himself and sat looking at all his wealth saying, "I'm all right for years and years." But God said to him, "You fool, tonight you will die, and although you are rich you cannot take it with you."

That is how it is for the man who gets loads of money, he may be rich, but in the eyes of God he is poor.

Moral

The moral of the story is that great wealth and power can cause people to forget that they are still ordinary human beings, and when they are ill or die money is no use to them. Unfortunately not everyone has understood this message and people still worship money despite knowing the evils it can cause.

Money, money, money

I'm always amazed when wealthy people become ill or the lives of their loved ones are threatened, they always seem to say that they would give up all their money and world-ly possessions to get them back or get them better.

Something else that often happens is that when a person is very rich the people around them usually can't wait for them to die to see what they've been left in the will. Some will even allow their greed to get the better of them and try to kill the person in order to get their hands on the money.

When you come to think of it ninety-five per cent of rob-beries, murders and assaults are motivated by money; sometimes for millions, sometimes for a few coins. So if money wasn't given such importance in our lives there would be much less crime, heartache and unpleasantness associated with it and a lot more peace of mind.

Spend, spend, spend

As soon as some people get hold of money they want to spend, spend, spend. But remember when you have money you don't have to spend it. Nowhere is it written that you've got to spend all your money as soon as you get it. The secret is to spend your money when you really need to. The best thing to do is to save it so you never have to borrow. Many people nowadays spend money they haven't got, they use credit cards to buy the things they desire because it seems so easy. They can get what they want instantly without having to save up for it. They always seem rather surprised when they have to pay it back with high interest.

Remember you never get something for nothing, there's always a price to pay. So make sure you know the cost of what you are letting yourself in for so that you don't get into a spiral of debt. Being rich isn't necessarily lots of fun; it can also bring a lot of heartache. A lot of rich people worry all the time about holding on to all their possessions and keeping up all the payments on their mansions, cars and other belongings.

If you have got money to spend, here are a few tips on how to spend it wisely.

1. If you are buying something, shop around and make sure you get the best price. Never buy the first one you come across.

2. Ask yourself if you really need it, or is it just a fad, something you want to impress your friends with.

3. Don't just spend your money because you've got it. It won't burn a hole in your pocket, save it for when you really need it.

4. Don't think that because something is expensive it will be good. Make sure you spend your money wisely and get good value for it. A lot of so-called designer clothes and luxury goods are just cheap things with

expensive labels. Don't fall for them.

5. Don't use money to buy friendship, buying expensive things for your friends will get you nowhere. When your money runs out so will your friends.

6. Don't gamble your money away, put it in a high interest savings account if you want to win every time.

Payoff

Whenever I see people with big flashy cars and lots of jewellery and clothes, I always wonder what bad things they have done to get them or whether they have got themselves deep in debt just so they can look the part.

People can be tempted to do anything for money but it can ruin their lives. Those who sell themselves are never happy because deep down they know they've done wrong. A gangster I once met said to me, "Everyone has their price." I said to him, "Yes, but if you sell yourself you'll have to live with a price tag around your neck for the rest of your life." So before you sell yourself for whatever reason ask yourself, "Is money really going to be the answer, is it going to make me happier and if so for how long?" You'll find that something you have saved up for and worked hard to get is far more rewarding than something you have stolen or something you have sold yourself to get. Don't be forced into the habit of thinking that everything has to come easily or instantly and that includes money.

One sure fire way to get on the slippery slope is to start gambling. For young people it may start with fruit machines. You may think fruit machines are an innocent bit of fun but they are not, they are a form of gambling and are cleverly designed to take your money away from you. You can easily become obsessed with these machines and find yourself doing anything to get the money to pour into them. Once you start you get hooked and you will find it hard to stop.

Believe me, you can never win. You might win at first and be tempted into thinking you can beat the machines but don't be fooled. When you go back the next time you are very likely to lose all your money. The only people who make any money are those who own the machines.

You may be one of the ninety-nine per cent I mentioned earlier who want to be rich. Sadly not everyone can be rich, the only answer is for the rich to get poorer and the poor to get richer so that everyone can have a bite of the riches. Unfortunately that will never happen mainly because of people's greed. What you have to do is not crave money and the short-term pleasures it brings.

That can be hard to do because everywhere you look you see a world slowly divided into two halves, those with money and those without. Every day you witness the importance that's put upon money and you can grow up with the belief that money is the only thing that will bring happiness.

One of the oldest sayings in the book is that "Money isn't everything", and it really is true. No matter what you see before you or what you are tempted to do to get it, keep telling yourself that money isn't everything! It will take more than money to make you truly happy.

I hope one day everyone will realize that there are more important things in life than money, like love and health, spiritual belief and contentment, these are the things that bring true happiness. To possess all these will make you one of the richest people in the world.

Dear Floella,

There was a girl in my class. Her nick-name was Pleasure because she used to come into school each day half an hour late for school and she would come in with something brand-new. Like the latest trainers or a gold chain or something new. One day she was having an argument with a girl and because she thought "Well I have a reputation so I am going to beat the girl up" and she did, at home time. She started to fight the girl and all Pleasure's friends were there watching but the other girl grabbed onto Pleasure's hair. Pleasure was losing and her brand-new bag burst at the strap and all because she thought she had all the best stuff. But one day her mum stopped buying things for her because people always broke her brand-new things.

Jason O'Connor

Dear Floella,

When I was in Primary School, there was a boy who used to show off by bringing new books to school every week. Everybody hated him for his habits. One day he was playing football and he put his bag on the grass and all the books were in it. He forgot about it and somebody came from the street and stole the bag then ran away. The boy was left with nothing and his parents told him that he wouldn't have anymore books bought for him due to his carelessness. The boy was left with nothing and he had to find another school because nobody wanted him for a friend because he was a show off. When he went to another school he didn't do the same. He behaved properly and that shows that showing off to people ends with nothing but evilness.

Mohamed Musa

Chapter 5

It's cool to be cruel?

B ULLYING OFTEN APPEARS IN THE NEWS, especially when a youngster is driven to commit suicide by the harassment and teasing of his or her classmates. What a thing for a bully to have on his or her conscience.

But why do people, especially kids, become bullies? Well often they are not happy with their own lives and they take it out on others who are weaker than themselves. By tormenting someone else they are simply covering up their own unhappiness. Perhaps they are unhappy at home and are suffering abuse and neglect or maybe they are not clever at school and no one likes them so they figure if they can't make people like them they can at least make people scared of them. Low self-esteem and jealousy are very common reasons why people bully. So behind the toughness the bully is saying, "I hate myself and hurting someone else makes me feel better".

So how do you defend yourself if you are being bullied? The Bible says "turn the other cheek". Well in this day and age it's not quite that straightforward. It's better to learn how to avoid a situation where you have either to defend yourself or turn the other cheek. Not everyone is able to fight or outwit the bullies, after all if they could they wouldn't become a target in the first place, would they?

Bullies at the gate

In this Bible story a whole city is threatened by bullies. The people dealt with them by being steadfast and not giving in to the threats and intimidation. They also had faith in their God.

The city of Jerusalem was surrounded by the

Assyrians, who had attacked and destroyed many cities and killed thousands of people. They had a reputation as the most feared and cruel fighters around.

The people of Jerusalem were terrified and they locked themselves inside the walls of their city. They could see thousands of fierce looking Assyrian soldiers camped below the city.

Then King Hezekiah of Jerusalem spoke to the people. "Don't be scared," he said, "Be strong and remember if we have faith in God no harm can come to us. God is our strength against these bullies."

Soon the Assyrian commander came out and shouted up at the gates of the city, "Your King Hezekiah is wrong. Don't believe him. Your God will not protect you against our swords and spears. We will simply wait out here until you starve to death! If you surrender and come out we will let you eat the fruit which is growing on your trees and drink the water from your wells." King Hezekiah and his people did not answer. Instead the king sent his officials to see the prophet Isaiah, to ask his advice. Isaiah sent back a message saying, "Don't let the Assyrians scare you. God will protect you and very soon they will leave you alone." So King Hezekiah prayed to God and asked for his protection from the Assyrians. That night the army received news that Assyria was under attack and the next day the Assyrian army was gone. The people of Jerusalem threw open the city gates and danced with joy. " Thank you, God," they said. "You have saved our lives."

Moral
In the story the people of Jerusalem decided to stand up to

the Assyrians who were threatening them. They got their courage from their faith in God. If you are being bullied and threatened you must find the strength to stand up to it. You may need someone to help you find that strength but the only way is to be strong.

Ten ways to beat the bully

It's not always easy to beat the bully but what you have to do is try and outwit them, try and think ahead. Be prepared to foil their wicked actions.

1. Try to avoid trouble spots, such as places the bully hangs out. If you have to pass there don't go on your own, or try to get there before them.

2. Don't attempt to "get in" with the bullies to try and get them to like you. It won't work, you will just become an easy target for them; it's best to avoid them.

3. Try to show a sense of humour when you get teased, and bullies will soon get fed up when they realize you won't take their bait.

4. Bullies are often jealous, so the bully is showing that he or she feels inferior to you, they are actually flattering you! So don't let them shake your confidence.

5. Bullies like to see you getting upset, if you cry or try to hit out they will be happy. The best thing to do is smile, even though inside you might be scared or really hurt. It takes real effort, but be strong.

6. You might get teased because of the way you look, but remember the story of the ugly duckling that grew into a beautiful swan. That could be you one day and then they will all want to know you.

7. You can win the bully over. If you are strong and show true strength of character they might eventually start to respect and admire you because they might begin to realize what they are doing is wrong.

8. Don't act superior and arrogantly, especially if you're clever. This will attract trouble and encourage bullies to pick on you.

9. Take a good look at yourself in the mirror and ask, "Am I making myself a target?" Maybe that lime green bobble hat you wear all the time is asking for trouble.

10. Most importantly, tell someone! Talk it over with someone who you trust, that includes parents, teachers, ministers, doctors, even your local policeman. They can help you. Get your school to talk about bullying in assembly or during religious studies. Do role playing in class which will show bullies what misery they cause and also teach you the skills you need to avoid trouble.

You can rest assured, one thing that has changed in the last few years is people's attitude to bullying. Nowadays it is taken very seriously indeed by teachers and adults. If you ask a teacher or an adult for help the chances are you will get it. If you don't, that person is irresponsible and is not doing their job properly!

What to do if you are being bullied

Firstly, ask yourself are you being bullied or just being teased. If you are an only child you will not be used to the playful teasing and rough and tumble with brothers and sisters which is a normal part of family life. This behaviour can help you to learn how to handle teasing and how to take care of yourself both at school and in the outside world. So if you are an only child, at school you might mistake teasing for bullying.

If you are called silly names at school don't take it to heart. Think of it as a bit of fun and try to think of a few silly names yourself. Have a good laugh instead of getting upset. You may find that things soon settle down and that you are quickly left alone. Of course if it does turn into real bullying then you must do something about it. Please don't be tempted to play truant from school to keep away from the bullies. You will be the loser in the end because not only will you miss out on your valuable schoolwork but you will also never learn how to face up to bullying and how to deal with it.

I've already told you ten ways to beat the bully but if none of them work and you feel you can't take any more you must immediately speak to an adult who will know how to deal with bullying. If you've told them once before and nothing has changed then tell them again or talk to someone who will take you seriously.

Don't blame yourself for what's happening to you and feel you have to end it all. What will that prove? You won't be around to see the results, those who care for you will be broken-hearted and worst of all the bully will have won and will go on to bully someone else. They might feel sorry for what they have done but that won't bring you back.

Find a way to get to grips with the situation, be strong because your strength will help you to be successful in later life and help you to cope with trouble.

Don't think that you are being a tell-tale if you report bullies or that you will get into trouble if you face up to the evil bully. You may feel your parents will over-react if you tell them you are being bullied. That's only natural because they love you and want to protect you, so let them know what's going on sooner rather than later. Talk it over with them calmly and don't feel you are putting extra worries on them. They will be far more worried if they find out the hard way.

Even if it ends up with you having to change schools it's better than suffering. The bullies may have won the first round but only time will tell what consequences they will have to pay. What you have to do is to believe in yourself, take positive action to stop what's happening to you and talk to someone. Remember talking over your worries can get results.

How to stop yourself being a bully

Are you a bully? Do you want to stop, but can't?
Ask yourself these questions and try to answer them honestly and truthfully from the bottom of your heart:

Do you think bullying is fun?

Do you think helping people weaker than yourself is soppy?

Do you find yourself being left behind with classwork?

Do you think bullying affects a person's happiness?

Do you feel unhappy because you are neglected and abused?

Does bullying people make you feel good?

If you have answered "yes" to any of these questions then you need to seek help. Perhaps you are being hurt deep inside and cannot do anything about it. You may be feeling guilty about what's happening to you so you try to cover it up by venting your anger on others. If you are, then you must find the courage to talk to someone about what's happening to you. Someone who can help put a stop to it and make you feel better about yourself. It's not your fault you are being abused or neglected, whoever is doing it to you is the evil one. They are evil not only because they are hurting you but they are also causing you to hurt and ruin the lives of others. So only you can stop the vicious circle because if you don't stop it now you could grow up and continue bullying and hurting people, even your own children and those you love. Now is the time to stop bullying before it's too late.

If the reason for you being a bully isn't abuse or neglect then ask yourself why you are doing it. If it's because you can't keep up in class then ask your teacher for extra help. Don't feel embarrassed about others laughing at you and thinking you are stupid. What you have to do is to start learning and understanding what you are being taught. When you do you'll soon begin to feel good about yourself and stop hurting others. Not everyone can be top of the form so don't feel bad if you're not. Try to discover what you are good at and work at it so you can stop bullying.

You may not realize it but that feeling of excitement you get from bullying and being cruel will be replaced by an even better feeling of accomplishment.

Be a guardian angel

Do you really want to be a bully and hurt others? Deep down in your heart you must know hurting others is wrong. Why not try going for a conversion? Try to convert yourself into a guardian. A guardian is someone who protects and cares for those who are weaker than themselves. The reward for being a person who is kind and protective to those weaker than themselves is a great feeling of self-worth and inner confidence. People may not come up to you and slap you on the back and say, "Hey, well done, you are a really good person," but they will think it and inside yourself you know that instead of hurting someone and making their life miserable you have done the opposite. You have given someone friendship and kindness and made them feel better, and as a result you will feel better. So if you are a bully turn your strength, power and energy into doing good and showing kindness.

Dear Floella,
It was my first day at secondary school and my mother had taken me to school. When I got inside the building I saw a lot of children staring at me. I got very frightened. My mother said that she had to be going now because she had to go to work and she never wanted to be late.

It was now break time and everyone rushed outside and into the dinner hall. So I rushed to the dinner hall to get my dinner ticket. But the dinner lady told me I couldn't have a ticket. So I went back outside where 3 big girls came up towards me and they started to bully me and told me to get money for them so I ran away and told a teacher . And when I got home I told my mother.

The next day I was back at school, the 3 girls never troubled me again.

Loreen Martin

Dear Floella,
One time in my class at primary school there was a bully.

He used to tease me about my name and bully me to do things, say things and go places for him. He used to punch me for no apparent reason. He even threatened me with a knife. Then one morning he came in as usual but different, he never made a joke about me. Earlier in the day I heard he got beaten up himself. I went over to him and he put his hand out, I put my hand out and shook it and we were friends.

I thought it better to be friends than to be enemies.

Liam Burke

Dear Floella,
*Last year I was being bullied and I used to
get very upset when this person used to say
things to me. I used to keep it to myself but
now if someone bullies me I tell the teacher.
Then the person who was bullying me
would get get into trouble.*

Sharon Howes

Dear Floella,
Last time I was bullied I never liked it. He
used to take my money or beat me up. This
carried on for a month until one day he
came into school and I picked up a chair and
hit him on the head and after all that I was
the one who got in trouble, not him.

Michael Nash

Dear Floella,
One day all my family was moving into a
new house. I could not wait because we
used to live in a hotel. That was not so good.
When we got there my mum said "do not
make friends with anybody round this area"
but I did not listen. There was this boy called
Mark who lived across the road from me.
One day I started to talk to him then I said
"no why should I shut my mouth". Then he
came across the road and started showing
off to his friends, teasing me . Then he
asked me for some money, if I did not give
him any he would beat me up. Then I told
my mum and she went over to his house
and told him off. From that day I did not talk
to him.

Kelly Edionseri

Dear Floella,
When I was in primary school there was a
boy called Dennis. He thought that he was
strong and bad. He bullied and teased
everybody in the class, he told me to give
him my dinner money or he will beat me up.
This went on for three weeks until I told my
mum what was going on. She came up to
the school and told the teacher that a boy
was taking people's dinner money. The boy
got told off and he got in trouble and he
had to pay back the money what he took
from people.

Wayne Stewart

Chapter 6

*Finders keepers,
losers weepers?*

I SUPPOSE EVERYONE at some stage in their lives is tempted to steal something. In fact there are few people who can honestly say they have never stolen anything. The problem is, some people go on to make a career of it, they can't stop and it becomes a habit. Many children never realize that stealing is wrong, they have no idea of the amount of pain and suffering it can cause.

Stealing often starts off quite innocently when you are a child. You may take something small like a sweet or some money and if you are asked if you took it you may be frightened to admit that you did, so you say "no". You weren't caught so you may feel a little excited about getting away with it or even think it's okay to steal. So you do the same thing again, and again, and again, not thinking about the wrong you are doing but only of the thrill of getting away with it.

But stop and think for a moment; that object, that money, that book, those trainers or that piece of jewellery you stole belonged to someone. How do you think they felt when they realized that it had gone forever? How would you feel if it was you who had had something stolen? I tell you it really hurts and the pain stays with you. Your thrill and excitement, your wrongdoing is someone else's grief.

When you steal something from someone it has a deep and lasting effect on them. But thieves rarely understand how sickening it is for someone to find that a thief has been in their home and ransacked it or to discover that someone has taken the car they worked so hard to buy and driven it to destruction. It's often not the material loss that hurts most but the emotional feeling of being mugged, robbed or burgled.

Excuse me

The excuse many thieves give for stealing is that their victims can afford it and have insurance anyway! But the truth is that most people have worked very hard to buy the things in their homes and some of them may not be insured. Their possessions may be of great sentimental value, gifts from parents or grandparents, irreplaceable things which when stolen leave the victim in great distress and with a deep sense of loss!

If only those who steal could realize how deeply they hurt people by invading their homes and stealing their treasured belongings. They might think twice before doing it and they wouldn't make excuses!

Lead us not into temptation

Every day of our lives we are faced with temptation. The temptation to steal is one of the strongest and if you are not made aware that what you are doing is wrong at an early age, the consequences of your actions will continue to hurt your victims every time you steal.

But how do you fight temptation? Well, as I said before, you must practise putting yourself in the place of the person you are stealing from. Ask yourself, "Do they need it more than me ? Do I need it ? Why am I doing it ? Is it for my own greed or to prove something to my friends?" Whatever the reason, DON'T DO IT! Let's face it, you might get caught and have to face the penalty. Think of the consequences; you will have hurt those who care for you, the victim and most of all *yourself* because in the long term you'll live to regret it. You could find yourself living a life of crime, in and out of prison for the rest of your life. Your freedom will have been stolen from you. So before you steal from others, think of the consequences.

The shirt

This is a story from India and it tells of a man who stole from another only to realize that his victim was even poorer than himself.

One night a man called Junaid Gaghdadi was saying his prayers as he always did. As he prayed a thief crept in through the open door and began to look around for something valuable to steal. Although Junaid was aware that a thief had entered his home he continued to pray. Junaid was not a wealthy man and all the thief could find that was worth stealing was a shirt, so he stuffed it into his bag and left. All the while Junaid had remained deep in prayer.

You see Junaid figured to himself that the thief must be really desperate for a new shirt if the only way he could get one was by stealing it. So he kept the theft a secret.

A few days later Junaid was in the market place when he came across two men who were arguing. Junaid stepped between the two men and asked why they were quarrelling. One of the men explained that he wanted to buy a shirt from the other but that he wanted proof that it wasn't stolen property. Junaid looked at the shirt in question and saw it was the one that had been stolen from him. Instead of calling for the thief to be arrested, Junaid said he knew the seller and that he would verify that the shirt was not stolen, then he even offered to buy it. Seeing the chance of a bargain slipping away the man hurriedly paid for the shirt and went on his way.

Of course the thief realized that Junaid was the one he had stolen the shirt from and he remembered that Junaid was a poor man. Yet he had not told anyone about the theft. The thief began to feel very guilty about his action and he felt ashamed of what he had done. He fell on his knees and begged Junaid's forgiveness and from that day on he never stole again. Junaid had by this simple action caused a fellow man to change from wrongdoing to the right path.

Moral

This is an ancient story and yet it has a modern message. Those who steal rarely realize the effect or consequences of their actions. You see many victims of robberies aren't rich people who can afford it!

How to stop stealing

If you really want to stop stealing then you have to have a plan to put into action and keep on practising it. The plan is to set out some rules which you have to recite or think about every time you feel the temptation to steal something. Here are a few suggestions for you to start with:

1. Imagine the thing you treasure most is stolen. That's how your victim will feel.

2. Keep telling yourself, "The price you have to pay in the future will be much dearer."

3. Remember the buzz you get from stealing will soon

disappear when you get caught and earn yourself a criminal record.

4. When you are about to steal something, put your hands in your pockets and say to yourself, "I'm not going to do it!"

5. Get your teacher to hold a discussion in class about stealing. Many young people have never discussed the subject, it may change a few people's way of thinking.

6. If you steal something, every time you look at it or use it you will remember that you stole it. It's much more satisfying to get things honestly, even if you have to work and save hard to get them.

Right and wrong

The way the world is going these days is very worrying indeed. People no longer have any morals. That means they don't care about the consequences of their actions. If it simply becomes a free-for-all where people just take what they want, where the strong take from the weak and no one cares how much crime there is, it's a terrifying future.

If people are terrified to leave their homes for fear of being mugged or returning to find their houses ransacked, if high street shops become fortresses against ram raiders and shoplifters, we will be living in a self-made hell. A sick world where there is no future for you, your children and your children's children.

Unless we start to understand and know the difference

between right and wrong, we are all in big trouble. Think about it!

Dear Floella,
My brother went to steal a pen and some
sweets from Woolworths. The pen he stole
was a black and gold Parker. As he started
to walk out of the shop, the manager
stopped him and took him into the office
and called the police. The manager told
them what he'd done then they took him in
the police van and brought him home and
told my mum and dad what he did. They
went mad.

Adam

Dear Floella,
When I was in my first year I was walking across the playground when I saw two boys having a fight one of the boys was in my class. While he was fighting he dropped £2 . He didn't know he had until the fight was over. He walked off. When he had gone I went and picked up the money. Later in class I saw the boy I asked him what was wrong, he said that he had lost his dinner money and his bus fare to get home. I felt guilty and gave it back.

John

Dear Floella,

I was out with my friends and one of them suggested that we go to the Prep-School and steal some tennis balls. When we got there the gate was unlocked and we went over to the roof and climbed on but there were no tennis balls. So we looked around the school and there was a door open and my friends went in. A few minutes later they came running back with a radio and a man chasing them. We ran but the man caught one of my friends. We gave ourselves up and were taken home by the police.

Michael

Dear Floella,

I went swimming once and was there for a long time . Afterwards I was so hungry I wanted something to eat but I did not have any money. I went into a shop and saw lots of drink and chocolate just lying there so I put some in my bag. I was about to go out when someone put their hands on me it was the store detective. I had to wait for my mum to pick me up. She went mad and was very angry with me. So she bought me about six cans of cola and ten chocolate bars and said I had to finish all of them. I felt like crying.

June

Chapter 7

Is hate great?

Q: WHO'S THE ODD ONE OUT?

A: NO-ONE IS

WHY DO PEOPLE hate each other? I'm not talking about hating one particular person, I'm talking about hating a whole group of people. It's called racism and it means hating people because of the colour of their skin, because of where they come from or even because of their religion.

I think a lot of racism is based on fear. The fear of something we don't understand, of something that is different from ourselves. It's part of human nature to be afraid of things we don't know about or understand and when we are afraid we get angry. We turn that anger into hatred and try to destroy what we hate so that we can feel safe. People of different races or cultures are sometimes difficult to understand so … we hate them. These ugly and primitive feelings have no place in the modern world and we must banish them from our hearts.

The secret is to start to understand other people and what makes them tick. To put yourself in their place so that you can imagine what it must be like to be them.

Everyone on this earth has a right to be here and a right to lead a happy life. The problem with humans is that no one has yet worked out a way of getting us all to live together in peace and harmony. Our quest is to find the key which lies somewhere in a deep dungeon. It is a golden key which will unlock our hearts and open our eyes so we can see each other as fellow humans.

Love your neighbour

I talked to a girl recently, a white girl called Denise. She told me that she had been hanging out with a group of other girls who were always talking about how much they hated black people, they wouldn't have anything to do with the black girls in the school. One particular black girl, Jasmine, who lived a few doors away from Denise was always getting picked on and called names by the others and Denise of course joined in. Jasmine stood up for herself but Denise could see it was making her life miserable.

One day Denise arrived home from school to find her mother was seriously ill and needed urgent medical attention. Denise ran to the next door neighbours but they were out so she went to Jasmine's house. When Jasmine's father heard what had happened he rushed to Denise's mother and gave her the kiss of life, and as a result she survived until the ambulance arrived. Jasmine and her mother took care of Denise and gave her some food and she stayed the night with them.

The next day at school Denise arrived with Jasmine. The other girls began to jeer and call Jasmine names as usual but now Denise felt differently, she felt angry and disgusted that they could be so ignorant. For the rest of the day Denise stayed with Jasmine and soon she began to realize that Jasmine was a really lovely friend. The others sneered at her for being with a black person but Denise didn't care. As the weeks passed Denise became close friends with Jasmine and her family and she soon realized that her racism was really a case of ignorance.

Denise told me that once she had got to know a black family she found that they were like any other family. Actually they were a very special family because they were responsible for saving her mother's life. Even though they knew Denise was part of the group at school who were calling their daughter names they did not let that stop them from helping her. They taught Denise a very valuable lesson by practising what the Bible says, "Love thy Neighbour".

Challenging hatred

Many people who are racist have never had much to do with the people or race they actually hate. They don't know why they don't like them, the thought has never occurred to them. They would probably come up with some silly reasons which they may not have found out for themselves but have heard from other people. Children can be influenced from a very young age to hate people of different colour and culture so they never get the chance to find out for themselves what different people are really like.

If you feel hatred for someone or a group of people even though you don't know them personally then you should do something to stop this evil poison taking over your mind, body and soul.

Every time you see those you hate or are reminded of them you will get a twisted feeling inside which will make you want to cause harm rather than doing something good. All right, you may get a thrill from knifing someone or beating them up or making their lives a misery. But sit down for a while and truthfully ask yourself why you are doing these wicked deeds. Could it be because you feel as if you have something to prove, you want to let everyone know you are better than those you hate? If you really were better than them you wouldn't need to shout about it or attack people to let them know, would you?

The reasons people give for hating other races are usually based on a complete lack of understanding and knowledge of the truth. Many of the answers are in the history books, you should take some time to read them. You'll find that people from different races helped to make countries like Britain, France, Holland, Spain and America rich over the centuries. Then they were invited to live, work and make their homes in the countries which they had helped to prosper.

Now that things have changed and they are no longer needed, they cannot just be told to go away. They have every right to share in what they and their forefathers helped to build. We all have to learn to live together instead of wasting energy hating each other, energy which could be put to much better use. The bad feelings that cloud your mind could be stopping you from doing something worthwhile. Hatred eats you up and takes you over, whilst being tolerant and understanding will make your heart swell with pride.

A good way to deal with racism is to ask yourself, "If we were all blind what would we hate each other for?" It certainly wouldn't be because of the colour of our skins! Something else to think about is, if you and someone you hate, for whatever reason, were suddenly confronted and challenged by an alien from another planet, which side would you be on? Would you stick with your fellow human, even though you belonged to a different race or religion or would you side with the alien?

Why wait for a tragic outcome to realize that we were all created on this planet, so we all belong on this planet. The earlier you learn to control and challenge hatred the better it'll be. No one is born with hatred in their hearts, hatred is learnt from others.

Let's take a typical school playground situation where a group of kids are making racist remarks about someone because of his or her colour or race. They will use certain words to describe them to put them down and you might find it's fun to join in too. You feel part of the gang, you get a feeling of belonging to a group … you even have a go at calling out a few names yourself just to show you're one of the gang. Before you know it you start thinking hateful thoughts and without realizing it you have become a racist. It's so easy. Pretty soon you can't even remember how it started, you just know you hate – you don't know why, you just do.

Feed my coat

One day a farmer of good standing was invited to a fine banquet at the home of a local nobleman. All day as he worked in his fields he was looking forward to the good food and conversation that lay ahead of him. So hard did he work though that he lost track of the time until suddenly he noticed it was getting dark. He realized he was going to be late for the banquet. There was only one thing to do, he would have to go straight there in his working clothes instead of going home to get changed into his best clothes.

When he arrived at the nobleman's house the rest of the guests had already arrived. As the farmer mingled amongst them he noticed that no one paid much attention to him. No one attempted to hold a conversation with him and the nobleman himself totally ignored him. When they sat down to eat the farmer was placed at the far end of the table, at the opposite end to his host. Without saying anything the farmer slipped away from the dinner table and made his way quickly home.

He washed and shaved and changed into his best clothes, over which he put on his finest most richly embroidered coat. He hurried back to the noble-man's house and entered the dining room grandly. The guests all looked at him admiringly and the nobleman leapt to his feet to greet him and ordered the servants to set a place by him for the new guest. Plates of tasty food were brought as the nobleman and several of the guests chatted with the farmer.

To their amazement the farmer, instead of eating the food began to stuff it into the pockets of his splen-did coat, saying, "Eat, my fine coat!" every time he stuffed something into a pocket! "What on earth are you doing that for?" asked the shocked nobleman. "Well," replied the farmer, "I'm simply feeding the guest you invited to dinner this evening. When I came here earlier in my working clothes you ignored me, but when I went home and changed into my finest clothes you treated me as if I were the most important guest here. But I am still the same person inside so it must be my fine coat you are so impressed by. So it should be the coat that gets the food, not me!"

Moral

The moral of the story is that people all too often judge others by their appearance and treat them accordingly. Rather than finding out about the person inside they make a quick judgment based on the outside.

How to beat the racist

The first weapons you need to beat the racist are self-esteem and self-confidence. Feel proud of your existence and don't let anyone convince you that you are not an important person. Tell yourself that if you were not hated for your colour it would probably be because of your accent or your religion, a racist will always find something to pick on. Don't try and change who you are or what you are, you will only end up confusing your own mind and then the racist would have won.

You can beat the racist by showing them that they cannot get to you. If you come from mixed-race parents you may sometimes feel very confused and vulnerable about who you are and allow others to upset you. But all you have to understand and say to yourself is that you are black and white mixed together which makes you golden and very special. Gold is a precious thing and so are you! You have the gift to understand what it's like to be black and white, so use it by learning about each culture.

Even though neither side might accept you, in the eyes of most people you will be considered black and you must never deny that fact. You must feel proud to be black just as you are proud to be white. If you continue to show this inner strength, this confidence, this sense of wellbeing, then people will soon realize they can't get the better of you. What you will have is a rich, full life which they will miss out on.

Whatever mixture you are, feel proud of it and discover the background of both your cultures. Never be ashamed of who you are. If you stand up to the racists and show them that you don't have to prove anything, that you believe in yourself and feel good about yourself, you never know, they might just try to get to know what's so special about you, and even wish they were like you! So remember you are special no matter what colour you are!

Dear Floella,
Do you think that people should be racist?
Someone got killed because they were
black. He was at the bus stop with his
brother and he saw some white boys and
they started to call him names then he said
it back then they came over and killed him.
Stabbed him in the neck he died instantly.
Killed because he was black

The end,

Roxanne Chin

Dear Floella,

Someone that I know says that where he lives in Elephant & Castle that he always gets called names because he is black. Every shop he goes to the shop owners always called him names. My friend's family went into the shops and asked them to stop calling him names. If you don't we will get you to court. Later in the week they did stop calling my friend names.

Ryan McFarlane

Dear Floella,
There was an African family moving into a
house next door to me. They had only been
there for one day. Lots of people were
calling them Arabs. Some of the family
came out of the door but when they tried
to get past the people beat them up. Ten
minutes later the people picked up bricks. I
knew what was going to happen next so I
ran to the phone and dialled 999 and told
the police the address. I heard smashing
noises outside. The police came round to
the house in a big van and caught everyone
who started the trouble. As soon as the van
went they asked who phoned the police, I
said I did they said "Thank you". We shook
hands.

James

Dear Floella,
I am of mixed race and have experienced
prejudice, it was an isolated case but still I
was depressed about it. The thing that
depressed me most is that I am not in a
position to defend myself as I am disabled
and deprived of my freedom. Isn't that
enough for them? I wish they would think
of other people's feelings.

Nicola Cope

Dear Floella,

I remember when me and my two brothers were going to Macdonalds and we saw a big group of Bermondsey boys coming towards us so we crossed the road. Then one of them said "Oi monkeys, go back to your jungle. Does this look like Africa to you?" So my brother went across the road and started cursing them so one of them stabbed my brother so I started to cry. My other brother went to phone an ambulance. They came but it was too late. My brother died. The boys went down for 3 years.

Delena Stephens

Chapter 8

An eye for an eye?

REVENGE?

OR FORGIVENESS?

W HEN SOMEONE DOES SOMETHING to you that you don't like, usually the first thing you want to do is to get your own back. Hang on a minute though, maybe the person is only doing their job, like a teacher giving you detention. Or maybe the person who upset you did it without realizing it. Of course they may have deliberately gone out of their way to do something nasty to you just to hurt you. Whatever the reason, when it happens perhaps all you feel like doing is putting into practice the old saying "An eye for an eye and a tooth for a tooth".

You forget about the Bible saying, "Turn the other cheek". You feel that's for fools, all you want to do is get revenge and the satisfaction it brings. Who can blame you, we've all felt like that.

Sometimes the things the Bible says seem confusing and old-fashioned, but the amazing thing about the Bible is that it's really based on common sense and many of the things it says are as true now as they were then.

For example:

"Do not set yourself against the man who wrongs you. If a man wants your shirt, let him have your coat as well. If someone in authority makes you go one mile go with him two. Give when you are asked to give and do not turn your back on those in need."

In other words, sometimes you can win a battle by reaching out to the other person and instead of punching them in the face you shake hands with them. Suddenly all the hatred and anger will disappear and a new friendship based on understanding will be born. It takes a really big person to achieve this but believe me if more people tried it there would be a lot less war and fighting in the world

You see the trouble with revenge is that it's like a game of Ping-Pong. Someone does something to you, so you do something back, so they do something back, and so on, and so on. That's how wars start and continue for years and years. Hatred builds up and is passed on from generation to generation. There are parts of the world where hatred and revenge are so deep that people are killing each other for something that happened hundreds of years ago.

As I said before, it takes a really big person to walk up to an enemy and shake their hand and say let's stop fighting and hating each other and try to be friends. The Bible says "love your enemy" – what that means is instead of fighting fire with fire you can take away the fuel of hatred and the fire will go out. That really takes guts! If we don't start learning to do that, the human race will end up destroying itself.

Inner strength

One of the many ways you can develop inner strength is to learn to forgive people who upset you, it's an amazing feeling. It's a feeling which will make you smile to yourself. When you do something which you know is morally right, your self-esteem and confidence will grow and grow. You will start to feel ten feet tall and people will start to notice and look at you in a different way. Gradually you will develop into a new person, a stronger and bigger person who others look up to – try it, you'll be amazed!

Revenge – don't do it!

You may find yourself in a situation where you have to

stand up for yourself, so that you are not taken advantage of. Defending yourself may prove to be the only way out, but what you mustn't get led into is a situation where the conflict is ongoing and fuelled by the desire for revenge.

I remember when I was fourteen I felt that the whole world was against me, especially when people called me names because of my colour. I felt I had to get my revenge on them, so I was always fighting and lashing out.

One day a boy much bigger than me, started calling me horrible names and as usual I saw red. His face looked so ugly as he spat the words out at me while he licked a lollipop. I just had to get even, I had to get revenge. So I quite calmly walked up to him and stuffed the lolly down his throat. He started to turn blue right in front of me.

Suddenly, it was as if time stood still and a soft voice spoke to me, "Floella, why are you doing this? Can't you see it is he who has the problem, not you? You could end up killing him because of his ignorance. You know who you are, be proud of it and don't sink to his level. Forgive him because he's ignorant and stupid." I then pulled the lolly out of his throat, smiled at him and said, "Yes I know I'm black and I'm very proud of it thank you."

When I walked away from him I felt as if I'd seen the light and that light has stayed with me ever since. Whoever that boy was, to this day I remain grateful to him.

Special branch

Revenge and forgiveness is not always to do with physical violence, it's sometimes to do with how we behave toward one another. One of the most despised people in olden times was the tax collector, many would go out of their way to be horrible to him and would never dream of being kind to him. They saw this as the only way of getting revenge.

One day Jesus was in Jericho where a rich tax collector called Zacchaeus lived. Zacchaeus was a very short little man and a bit on the plump side and people were always poking fun at him. He was hated because not only did he collect taxes for the Romans but he also became rich by cheating his own people. When Zacchaeus found out Jesus was in town he rushed to the place where Jesus would be passing, but the roadside was already teeming with hundreds of people all anxious to catch sight of Jesus. Zacchaeus was far too short to see over the heads of the crowd and when they saw who it was trying to push to the front, they refused to let him get through.

Suddenly he had an idea, he ran ahead of the crowd and found a tree that overhung the road where Jesus would walk. He climbed up into the tree and sat on a branch.

As Jesus approached the branch where Zacchaeus was perched, to everyone's surprise he stopped and looked up at the little man. "Zacchaeus," he said, "Come down, I would like to stay at your house today." Zacchaeus almost fell out of the tree with shock.

Not only did Jesus call him by name but he was speaking to him nicely! No one had done that for as long as Zacchaeus could remember. That day Zacchaeus made Jesus welcome in his home. Many people were upset. "How could Jesus have anything to do with that little cheat?" they said.

That evening after dinner, Zacchaeus made a speech to a stunned audience. He admitted that he had cheated and taken money from his own people. But his meeting with Jesus had changed him. He swore he would never cheat anyone again. He promised to make amends and to give half his money to the poor and to repay those he'd cheated four times over!

Jesus smiled to himself. "A life has been saved here today. Zacchaeus has decided to live as God wants. This is why I came here, to look for those who have lost their way and bring them back to God."

Moral

The message is clear. Jesus showed Zacchaeus forgiveness, he reached out his hand in friendship and by doing so made Zacchaeus realize his cheating and sinful ways. Had Jesus ignored Zacchaeus like everyone else, he would have never changed.

Forgiving is not forgetting

If your heart and your head are full of revenge it will poison you and you could be the one who suffers by having evil thoughts.

So the next time you feel as if you want to get even with someone who has annoyed you, try to convert that evil thought into a positive one of forgiveness, try offering an olive branch in the shape of a sweet or a comic or even a joke.

Try to see things from the point of view of those who are annoying or upsetting you and forgive them, for they may not know what they are doing. Even if they do you must stand up to them with confidence and say, "This could go on for a long time so it's better to stop now before we waste a lot of time and energy." Rather than escalating the situation you have decided to defuse it.

Forgiving does not mean forgetting, it means that you

have been big enough to give the other person a second chance in the hope that they will learn a lesson. It may be that they are very unhappy people who are only accustomed to experiencing conflict and having bad things happen to them. So your gesture could be a turning point for them. Perhaps they could end up following your example. You may be worried that people might think of you as being weak, scared or chicken if you are able to forgive quite easily and don't take revenge. But don't feel like that, to be able to forgive is a sign of great strength not weakness. Instead of a burning angry feeling in your head and heart you'll get a glowing satisfied feeling of pride in yourself which will make you stronger.

Dear Floella,
One day I borrowed a computer from a
friend who lived next door. When I was
playing it, another friend came along and
asked if he could borrow it. I said "No!" The
next day I went to my gran's house for the
weekend. When he knew I had gone he
came to my house and told my mum that I
said he could borrow it. My mum gave it to
him. When I got back I found out what had
happened. I didn't forgive him at first but I
do now.

Christopher Docherty

Dear Floella,

My best friend stole my dress once. She did not ask me because she thought that I would not give it to her. She wore the dress to a party and I went to the same party and I saw her in my dress. I went up to her and she saw me. She started saying, "I am sorry forgive me please." She was asking for forgiveness but I did not forgive her. Then later I forgave her and we became friends again. Forgiveness is good.

Priscilla Oduro

Dear Floella,

There was a boy who used to bully me and I always ignored it. Every day when I came to school he bullied me but I never said anything and everyday it got worse. One day he bullied me until I got angry and I suddenly took a chair and threw it at him. His face started to bleed and the matter was taken to the Head. I explained what happened and I was sent to the class again. The boy was taken to hospital and he was admitted. After two days in hospital I went to see him and I begged him to forgive me and he also begged me to forgive him. We became best friends and everybody was surprised.

Mohamed Musa

Chapter 9

Life takers

COCAINE, CRACK AND ECSTASY are all dangerous drugs that are affecting our society. More and more young people's lives are being ruined because of them and yet many take up drugs blindly, without realizing the dangers.

Any substance which has a dramatic effect on your body is potentially lethal. Glue sniffing is a killer and yet many youngsters do it without realizing the danger they are in. Smoking and alcohol come under this heading too. Even though cigarettes and alcohol are sold openly in shops they are just as lethal as the so-called hard drugs. The outcome of using them in many cases can be fatal.

Many of us take drugs as medicines for one reason or another. We take drugs like aspirins, cough medicines and hay fever tablets to help us feel better. When we are seriously ill, drugs can save our lives. But although drugs can be "life savers", when they are used wrongly they can be "life takers".

Special effects

Drugs affect you in two ways – they affect your body and they affect your mind. Firstly the effects on the body are dramatic. They can make you violently sick, give you a heart attack, slow down your breathing, make you drowsy and cause you to lose your appetite. These are just some of the short-term effects, the long-term effects are even worse. These effects at first may not be obvious because a young body is like a new car. If you drive a new car hard, don't service it, don't put oil in it and put the wrong petrol in it, being a new car it will continue to go for a while. But as the mileage gets higher things start to go wrong because the damage has been done. When you are young, your body can take an enormous amount of punishment and abuse. But like the car, it will eventually begin to show the strain, and things will start to go wrong. Gradually the side effects start to take their toll on the body. The heart, liver, kidneys, stomach, in fact every major organ in the body will begin to deteriorate.

The second thing that deteriorates is the mind. Many drugs have an effect on the natural functions of the brain and even after just a few uses the mind can become affected permanently. Drugs can cause hallucinations, confusion, depression and other mental problems. They can make you feel overexcited and out of control which can cause you to put yourself and others in danger. So remember, "Your body is a Temple". Keep it beautiful, don't abuse it and it should reward you with a long and healthy life.

Pal pressure

One of the main reasons for taking drugs is peer pressure. That means the people around you try to make you do things you might not want to do. Of course people who try to get you to do the same as them have a confidence problem. They need you to do it as well to support them so they don't feel alone or isolated. To be different takes a lot of strength of character, especially when your friends put you under pressure to try drugs. It takes a great deal of will power and mental strength to resist, and if you do resist, you could be made to feel like an outsider.

Don't be led astray, if your friends start using drugs, get new friends because if you don't, you too could end up taking drugs yourself. Curiosity may get the better of you and you might try out some drugs to see what effect they have on you. Before you do, look at those who have tried drugs. What has it done for them? Are they brighter and happier once the drugs have worn off? Or do they have to keep taking more and more to stay high? Do you think the effect will be any different for you? No it will not!

Don't let them fool you into thinking that you can come off drugs whenever you want to. Remember for every high there is a price to pay. Don't become a "burn-out" like those who are encouraging you to be like them. They don't deserve your friendship.

Being pressurized to take up drinking can also be lethal. Many young people die as a result of alcohol poisoning, they simply drink too much, collapse and die. In some cases so-called friends have helped to kill them by encouraging them to pour alcohol down their throats. One of the most stupid things young people do is to spike other people's drinks with drugs and alcohol. They might think it's a joke but it can be a killer. So be on your guard against idiots who do this!

Drinking may feel like fun at first but most young people cannot control their drinking and don't know when to stop. Alcohol advertising tries to make drinking look exciting, glamorous and sophisticated, but no matter what the shape of the bottle, no matter what's on the label, be it wine, beer, whisky or vodka, it's all the same. It's just a drug called alcohol, so don't be fooled into thinking otherwise. It'll make you sick, stupid and dangerous! So don't let anyone force you into starting drinking.

No matter how cool, grown up and sophisticated your friends may think they look with a cigarette hanging out of their mouths, believe me they look like complete idiots!

Everyone knows they must be idiots because only a fool would pay to damage and destroy themselves after hearing all the evidence against smoking. Don't follow suit, because you think smoking makes you look good on the outside because it's doing you no good at all on the inside, in fact it will kill you! Smoking not only harms you by causing cancer, ulcers and heart disease, it harms innocent non-smokers who have to share the air around you.

Don't allow peer pressure to rule your life, and push you into doing things you don't want to do, especially when you know that it's wrong. Choose your friends carefully, search out those who feel the same as you do, and stick with them. Hanging out with the wrong crowd can lead you into trouble. Bad company means bad habits!

The Bible warns us against falling in with bad company:
"He who walks with wise men becomes wise, but the companion of fools will suffer harm."
(Proverbs 13:20)

Those who take drugs are fools, so don't mix with them and become a fool too!

Don't be pushed

If someone came up to you in the street and tried to kill you with a baseball bat you wouldn't like it would you? Drug pushers are doing the same thing, but they are trying to kill you with their drugs. It's not as obvious but they are trying to kill you just the same! They say things like "I've done crack and I'm OK, aren't I?" or "Only wimps don't take heroin," or "You can't criticize things unless you've tried them." What nonsense! You wouldn't try jumping out of an aeroplane without a parachute would you? You don't need to try things you know are very likely to kill you! Pushers try to make you feel as if you've missed out on something. You haven't. Appreciate the life you have been given and look after your body and keep it in good order. Taking drugs will not improve your life.

Saying "No"

Practise being assertive. Rehearse saying "No!" in front of a mirror. Have some phrases prepared for the moment of truth. Phrases like:
"I don't believe in body pollution."
"I'm proud of my body both inside and out."
"No, I don't want to."
"Do I look stupid?"
"No thanks, I know better."

Why some people are
tempted to say "Yes"

Some people are tempted to take drugs because life might not be going well for them. They might be feeling unloved and unwanted. Or they may be depressed because of schoolwork and the pressure of exams or sports and they believe drugs will help them perform better. At home, a family break-up or the death of a loved one can lead to a sense of loss or of not belonging which can lead them to turn to drugs.

Those who lack confidence might also be tempted to take drugs. To feel part of the crowd they may be tempted by their friends to join in with their drug taking. Whatever the reason saying "yes" to drugs isn't the answer. Whatever your problems are, drugs will only make them worse.

What you must do is believe in yourself and think positively and you'll be surprised how things will suddenly begin to look brighter. I always say, "Just as you're about to give up is the precise moment when things are about to turn around and come good." If you give in you'll never find out how good things could have been.

You should always remember that if you hide behind drugs you are sure to lose touch with reality and destroy the wonderful creation you have been blessed with – your body!

Try to keep your body healthy, fit and strong, free from drugs, alcohol and nicotine so that you can cope with the many challenges, battles, stresses and temptations life will throw at you. Remember a healthy body means a healthy mind.

Dear Floella,
There were two boys in my class, Mark and Gary. Before they met Gary was a good boy but one day Gary's mum walked into his bedroom and found the two of them smoking. She said, "What do you think you are doing? Mark I think you should go home right now. Before Gary met you he was a very good boy but now look at him smoking away in his room. Now go and I will ring up your parents and tell them what a silly boy you are. "Later that day Mark rang up and said to Gary, "I've given up smoking what about you. It will keep us out of trouble." Gary said he would never smoke again. So they never touched a cigarette after that ever.

Leanna Murphy

Dear Floella,
I was walking past some boys who were
smoking. I went up to them and one said,
"Hi, mate do you want a smoke?"
"No" I replied.
"Want some spliff?" "No" I said again.
"Alright, but you're missing out" said a
boy, "are you sure not even some pot?"
"OK," I said. A thing in my head said "No",
but I said "Yes". I had a puff and started to
choke I ran from them and got a headache.
When my Mum and Dad asked me what
was wrong I had to tell them. I was inter-
viewed by the police and was in trouble
with Mum and Dad. The dealers were
caught and I am never going to touch the
stuff again. I've seen some more gangs
smoking but I just say "No" but it's hard to.

Kevin

Chapter 10

Should you head butt your neighbour?

VIOLENCE IS WRONG and we know it. Unfortunately human beings are a very violent lot. Let's face it we've been killing each other since we first walked on the earth. It's no use just saying, "Well that's human nature isn't it? There's nothing we can do about it." I don't go along with that. What I say is that we are supposed to be evolving and that should mean becoming more civilized, less violent and more caring in everything we do.

In prehistoric times we had to fight to survive and unfortunately that instinct has stayed with us. We all feel as if we want to hit out at others from time to time, but if we gave in to those feelings every time we felt angry, we would be bashing each other's brains out all the time.

Everywhere you look there is violence; on television, in the movies, in the newspapers and right there in front of you, on the street and in the playground. It can erupt at any time, even at home.

Some of the worst forms of violence, such as stabbing and shooting are on the increase and it's not just adults who are committing these senseless acts. Children and young people are carrying knives and weapons and think nothing of using them even for trivial arguments. We often hear of young lives being tragically lost over minor incidents; people get stabbed because they accidentally knock into someone in the street or because they refuse to hand over their trainers or a few coins, they even get attacked because of their school uniform! Young people get stabbed and killed because of the colour of their skin. All pointless and senseless reasons for committing the ultimate crime of taking a life.

The trouble is that, as the saying goes, "violence breeds

violence", in other words, soon everyone will be carrying guns and knives to defend themselves. The only way to stamp out violence is by showing people that it doesn't pay and that it's socially irresponsible and immoral!

Crimes of our time

Mugging is a crime that has been around for centuries, it's only recently that we've invented a word for it, and it has become one of the most common crimes of our time. It's a horrible crime which leaves the victim both physically and mentally hurt. What people don't realize is that any physical attack leaves the victim with mental scars which take far, far longer to heal than physical ones. It's especially painful when old people are mugged, many of them are destroyed from the inside. They begin to feel inadequate, defenceless and helpless. That's just one form of violent crime of our time; there are many others which are just as ugly and cause terrible suffering for the victims.

Many very young children play at killing and hurting each other and sometimes don't realize that if they go too far their victim won't get up and come back to life again, like the characters in cartoons. This is one of the saddest crimes of our times. An innocent life has been lost forever and the ones who have taken that life will have to live with the most terrible guilt for the rest of their lives. You see, no one, no matter how young they are, can block out such an awful act. When they grow up and have their own family the memory of what they did will return, the slightest thing will bring back the horror and the guilt, a child playing in a playground or a screaming baby will trigger off the memory. So in a way those who commit such violent acts become victims themselves.

We must learn from an early age that it's very wrong to take a life and it is an evil crime to kill another human being.

Destroying property with fire is becoming more widespread amongst young people. They perform this violent act for several reasons, sometimes through curiosity to experience the sensation of a fire. But all too often they do not think of the consequences of their actions, the destruction they cause and the possibility of killing someone in the fire.

Another reason why people start fires is because of frustration and anger with the world and the people who hurt them. They see the fire as a way of symbolically getting rid of all the unpleasantness in their lives. They mistakenly believe that by burning a building their problems will go up in smoke too. In reality the act of starting a fire will only add to their problems. They will have a whole new set of problems when they get caught.

TV times

Some people may be influenced by the violence they see on television. What we have to remember is that a lot of what we see on television is nothing like reality. We have to realize that many of the things we see are just entertainment. They are acts which have been carefully scripted, choreographed and edited to look exciting. It wouldn't be exciting for the viewer if the actors chatted about their disagreement or cops and robbers discussed things in a civilized way. What the viewer wants to see is action, a few shoot-outs and lots of punch-ups! The trouble is the pictures are so powerful they may influence young people subconsciously.

Hi-Tech violence

Computer games are very popular with young people. They are technically very clever and brilliantly inventive, but the problem with them is that the most popular ones on the whole tend to be very violent. It is possible that they may influence the players into believing that the only way to solve problems is through violence. So when young people have to face real life confrontations they may resort to what, in their eyes, seems to get the instant result to a problem: violent behaviour. Children have always fought but not in the vindictive way that is becoming acceptable nowadays.

They may not realize it but subconsciously, violent behaviour is becoming the norm in their minds and computer games may help to enforce their perception of violence as acceptable behaviour. Computer games can be just as exciting, challenging and rewarding without being violent; like many things they can be used for good or evil, it's up to us to decide which.

Venting the pent-up anger

So why else is violence on the increase? Sadly we live in a world that makes people feel angry and frustrated. The trouble is that although we have created a world full of pressures, we have forgotten how to relax and get rid of our frustrations and anger in a non-violent and creative way. All our anger is pent up inside us, just waiting to explode.

For some a way of venting anger and frustration is to spray graffiti everywhere. They imagine that it will tell everyone how they are feeling, it's not as violent as punching someone's head in but it's just as destructive. It would be less hurtful to others if they tried to express themselves verbally, people might take more notice of what they're trying to say.

A lot of frustration arises when people don't know how to read and write properly, this can cause them to get angry inside and so lash out because they cannot understand the world around them.

They are locked inside a cage of ignorance and the only way out is through the door of violence. They use violence to hide their inadequacy and to try to make people respect them, to show that they are at least good at being bad! It's very hard for them to admit they have a problem with reading and it's often only when they end up behind bars that they start to seek help. But if only they could start improving their reading skills before it gets that far. If they could learn to read they could open up their minds to all the wonderful knowledge contained in books. They would begin to feel confident in themselves, become more tolerant and understanding and less violent.

The reality of violence

Whatever form violence takes it always leaves those who are involved feeling sickened and shocked. Films, television, computer games and comics give a totally false and unrealistic impression of violence. They glamorize it and make it look as if it's an easy and instant way of solving problems. What they hardly ever show is the long-term pain and suffering it causes. They never show the lingering pain of an injury or the suffering of someone who loses an eye or is permanently injured in some way. In films people get shot and surprisingly are up and fully recovered, with no lasting effects a few scenes later! It's not like that in real life, the human body is a delicately balanced and fragile thing and once damaged it takes a long time to heal, sometimes it doesn't heal at all. It's the same with the mind, it can be damaged by horrific experiences and frequently the effects last for life.

That's reality!

Street crime in the Bible

This is the story Jesus told of someone who is attacked by muggers and left bleeding at the side of the road.

One day a man set out to walk from Jerusalem to Jericho. Soon he left the town behind and he saw fewer and fewer other travellers on the road ahead. Suddenly a band of muggers jumped out from behind a rock. They beat him up, stole everything he had and left him half-conscious at the side of the road. Soon another man came walking along the road and although he was a priest, when he saw the man he glanced nervously around and walked quickly past on the other side of the road. He thanked his lucky stars it hadn't been him the muggers had beaten up.

Pretty soon another man who was a Levite and worked in the Temple came walking past, he looked at the injured man then he too crossed the road and hurried on his way. Then a third man came by, this time he was a Samaritan. (Now Jesus knew that Jews disliked the Samaritans and wouldn't even speak to them but that was part of the reason he was telling the story.)

The Samaritan saw the injured man lying battered and bruised at the side of the road. He took his saddlebag from his donkey, took out a bottle of olive oil and a bottle of wine and used them to clean the man's cuts. Then he gently lifted the man onto the back of the donkey and took him to a nearby inn where he found him a room. The Samaritan made the man comfortable and gave the innkeeper some money, saying "Take good care of this man and if you need any more I'll pay you when I come back this way."

Moral

In this simple story Jesus makes two important points. Firstly, that we must love one another, regardless of what race, colour or religion we are. Secondly, that it is the people who are kind and help others who everyone admires. No one remembers the muggers because no one has any respect for them and furthermore people who are violent will never have any respect for themselves. As they grow old they will never be able to forget the horrible things they have done, their crimes will haunt them for the rest of their lives.

Fighting violence

Aggressive and violent feelings are brought on by many things, some of them not as obvious as you might think. Food, believe it or not, can affect you and can make you feel very violent. If you suspect that something in your diet is affecting you, try leaving it out and see what happens.

Just simply growing up can cause you to have wild mood swings, hormones are being produced which can make you feel as if you want to lash out at anything that annoys you. Being pressurized at school or at home can make you want to take it out on someone. Brothers and sisters can sometimes drive you so mad that you end up in a fight. Being criticized or told off at school by your teacher can also bring on a nasty violent feeling.

Sometimes exploding violently seems to be the only way of expressing your frustration and anger but there are other ways of getting rid of those feelings. For example, tough physical sports like football, rugby, hockey, basketball, American football, volleyball, netball or even badminton will help you to let off steam. It doesn't mean kicking someone's head in and fouling them! What it means is playing a game aggressively in a controlled way. After the game you will find all your aggression is exhausted.

Believe it or not, contact sports like karate, judo, kendo, or even fencing are good ways to get rid of violent feelings. When you play these sports you gain confidence by controlling your body's strength which means you don't have to prove how tough you are on the street. It's a fact that people who are black belt karate experts are the least likely people to start a fight.

If you are not a sporty person you could try finding a secluded spot and yelling all your aggression out, it works wonders! Or just simply take a deep breath and count to ten whenever you feel violent. The worst thing you can do is store up your feelings of aggression, they will always find a way out so make sure it's in a way that doesn't hurt anybody!

If you are musical you could try forming a heavy metal group and letting out your violence as loud aggressive music. I guess being the drummer would be best! You never know you might end up becoming a rock star!

The thing is it's not very nice being involved in any kind of violence. In most fights there is a winner and a loser, somebody stronger beats somebody weaker. It's always a pity though when people start using violence to get what they want or to make themselves feel good by hurting those weaker than themselves.

I wish there was an easy way to make people understand that feeling good about being tough and violent isn't half as good as the feeling you get from being thought of as the kind of person who people feel safe around – the kind of person who will take care of those weaker than themselves. The respect people will give to that kind of person is enormous. You know the kind of person I mean, Hollywood films are full of them. Heroes and heroines who are really tough and strong, who are amazing fighters, who use their strength to protect those weaker than themselves, true Robin Hood characters.

If you're big and strong and a good fighter there are two things people might feel when they see you coming towards them in the street. They can think, "Oh no, here comes trouble!" or they can say, "Oh thank goodness, I feel safe now." It may feel good to make people scared of you but it's a real thrill to have people trust you and feel protected and safe when you're around.

Punchline

Any violent crime is an act of violence against yourself and society, as I said earlier, evil acts always return to haunt those who commit them. If you contribute to making the world a violent and frightening place, one day the violence will turn on you and you will be a victim.

It's often been said that we are now living in a civilized society. If we truly were it would be a society where people looked after each other and were not afraid of being attacked, robbed or beaten up. But nowadays that's far from the truth, many think nothing of hurting, maiming or even killing others because they feel violence is part of human nature. But isn't it about time we overcame our worst instincts and tried to be less violent towards one another! So the next time you feel like being violent and hurting someone, think again and let's make this a really civilized society ... please!

Dear Floella,
I was walking home from school and some
older boys started to follow me. Then one of
them tripped me up. I turned around and
said, "Why did you do that?" One of the
boys said , "What are you looking at?"
"You" I said and walked on.

Then one of the boys turned me around
and punched me. I punched him back really
hard and ran home.

Michael Norris

Dear Floella,
I beat my brother up for no reason at all. I
like calling him names like spastic and other
names like poof. He doesn't like that, that's
why I do it. My favourite time is when I
hit and kick him until he lets me play his
computer. I gave my brother two black eyes
for not letting me read his book. My
favourite name for him is spastic that gets
him really upset.

Mark

Chapter 11

Faith, hope and clarity

THERE IS NOTHING like the feeling of depression. We've all felt it at some time or another. The tiniest thing can spark it off. It can drag on for days and days. You feel really miserable and hopeless, you don't want to do anything and would rather slump in front of the television or just lie in bed. Nothing anyone says can make you feel better. Depression is probably one of the most common states of mind you can get into and when you get it there seems absolutely nothing you can do about it. Of course there are different types of depression, brought on by different things. It could be something as simple as not being chosen for the team, not getting a good mark in class or not being invited to a party. However, it could be something far more serious, a family break-up, not feeling loved and wanted, the death of someone close to you, being abused or being bullied at school or feeling a failure.

You may not think so but sometimes depression can be brought on by your surroundings. Dirty litter-covered streets or unpleasant living conditions can affect you quite badly. It has also been proved that some foods can have a depressing effect on you, as can pollution in the air. A long illness such as flu is another common cause of depression. Even long, dark winter nights can affect you, and doctors call this condition S.A.D. which stands for Seasonal Affective Disorder.

If you are born with some sort of disability, life at times may seem like an uphill struggle and can make you feel very depressed. You probably ask yourself time after time, "Why me, why am I in this position?" But have you thought of the fact that your purpose in life may be to teach others how to be considerate, understanding, thoughtful human beings. Each one of us has a purpose in life, don't think that you haven't and you are unimportant. Your purpose is to make others open their minds and eyes. Don't let depression cloud your thoughts and make you feel that you cannot contribute.

Depression can last for a few minutes or for days. However long it lasts it's never a pleasant experience. Depression is a perfectly normal state of mind if it lasts for a short period of time, after all you can't be grinning with happiness all day every day can you! Depression becomes worrying when it lasts for days on end. If all this makes depressing reading do not despair, there are ways to fight depression.

Have you got the blues?

Before you start to fight depression decide if you are truly depressed or just feeling down in the dumps. Do this by answering the following questions truthfully to yourself:

Do you feel as if you can't concentrate, especially at school?

Do you find that nothing is fun?

Do you feel tired and want to sleep a lot?

Do you wish you were somewhere else?

Do you feel sick all the time?

Do you always feel like crying?

Do you get angry quickly?

Do you feel like not eating much?

Do you feel like overeating?

Do you feel as if you hate everyone?

Do you find it hard to face life?

Do you feel nervous and get butterflies in your stomach?

If the answer to some of these is "yes" then it's possible you are suffering from serious depression and need help.

Don't despair – there are ways of fighting depression and there are people who can help, but most of all you can help yourself. What you must practise doing is having faith in your beliefs as well as yourself. Think positively, keep hope in your heart and things will become much clearer in your mind.

The boy who couldn't go to town

Sometimes you can get depressed if you are not allowed to do what you want to do. You may be told you can't do something for your own good by someone who loves you. They only say "no" to you because they care about you. This old Russian folk story illustrates just such a situation.

One day a boy's father was going into town.
"Please take me with you, Father," said the boy. His father shook his head, saying, "It's a long journey, stay at home." The boy felt sad and depressed. He burst into tears, hid under the stairs and cried himself to sleep. He dreamt about going off to town with his father along the path which led from their house to the town. He saw his father and ran after him until he

caught him up. They marched off together towards the town. When they reached the town they saw the baker baking bread rolls. "Please Father, buy me a hot bread roll," he pleaded.

When he woke up he realized his depression was only causing him to suffer. So he jumped up, put on his gloves and shoes and went outside. He saw his friends playing with sledges on the ice. He ran and joined them and played until he was tired. Eventually he made his way back to the house shivering but happy. When his father returned from his trip to town he said to the boy.

"I'm glad to see you have cheered up!"

The boy ran and hugged his father. "Did you buy me a bread roll?" he asked.

"Of course I did, my son." His father smiled and handed him the warm bread.

The boy felt so happy he jumped for joy.

Moral

The story is about a simple case of depression. The boy wanted to go to the town with his father because it was exciting and different but the father knew best, he knew that the journey was long and the boy would freeze. In other words he loved him and knew what was best for him.

As soon as his father went, the boy sank into a deep depression and curled up alone and slept (a typical symptom of depression). When he woke up though, he pulled himself together, went out to play and forgot his problems.

The moral is, sometimes you might have to do things you don't like but those who care about you usually know best and it will be better for you in the long run to listen to them.

So don't sulk, if you do only you will suffer. Instead try to find a way to get rid of the depression.

Self-help

You can always have a go at trying to overcome your depression by taking positive steps to change your situation. Just remember depression is the opposite side of the coin to happiness, so what you must do is flip the coin over.

Here are some tips to help you flip that coin and beat depression.

1. Force yourself to do something constructive no matter how small, like changing round your room, sorting out your belongings, writing a letter to someone, even yourself.

2. Take part in a charity event like a sponsored walk or swim or collect for a jumble sale or bring-and-buy sale.

3. Do something for someone else. This can make you forget your own troubles.

4. Check your diet and make sure you eat properly. Have a good breakfast, a healthy lunch and a nourishing main meal. Lay off the junk food and remember sweets can have a drastic effect on you. They can make your moods suddenly go up and then come crashing down.

5. Think positive thoughts. You can't be happy all the time, you have to have ups and downs. So tell yourself, "When I'm down the next thing will be an up!

The lower the down, the higher the up." So you've got something positive to look forward to

6. Don't set your goals too high, both at school and in play. If you set unrealistic goals you may not be able to achieve them.

7. Don't let friends and parents pressurize you into biting off more than you can chew, you'll only end up being unhappy if you feel you've failed them or yourself. Try to persuade them that you know your own limitations.

8. If someone is bullying you, annoying you or aggravating you take positive steps to change the situation by avoiding them or talking to someone in authority about it.

9. Take up a sport, do some exercise or dance to your favourite music to get the heart pumping and the blood moving. Remember a healthy body equals a healthy mind.

10. Have a good laugh! It may sound silly but laughter has a powerful effect on the soul. Listen to or watch tapes of comedy shows or simply have a joke telling session with your pals.

How to get help

As I said before, everyone gets depressed at some time and I have described some ways of dealing with depression. But if you still feel depressed after trying self-help and the feeling continues over a long period of time, then you have to seek help from someone like your family doctor as there could be a medical reason for your continual depression.

Family doctors are usually very reluctant to prescribe pills for depression as they can be addictive and don't really solve the root problem. So don't start taking any drugs you could get hooked on. For goodness sake don't start taking any uppers. Others who could help you are your parents and members of your family, like brothers and sisters, aunties, uncles or grandparents, your teacher or someone from your church. What you need is a good listener. There's an old saying which goes, "A problem aired is a problem shared" and it is so true. If you keep your thoughts locked inside you they will brew and fester making your life miserable. Try expressing how you feel. Doing this can lift the weight from your shoulders. Talking freely may not come easily at first but try to speak out gently, it may come out all jumbled, but slowly unload your thoughts and anxieties until you begin to feel lighter and unburdened. Sometimes you may even find that things aren't half as bad as you imagined. I always say that coming out of a depression is like the dawn rising.

Dear Floella,
My grandmother came to visit and she told
me what it was like at our old house and
that sort of stuff. The next day my mum said
gran was in hospital because of something
to do with her blood. I got very upset and
depressed because I didn't want her to die.
After a few days she finally came back and
that made me happy.

Ahmed Deria

Dear Floella,

I was on school holiday and some friends and I were supposed to go out for the day. We left at one o'clock and their mother was going to take us swimming. We were on the way when the car ran out of petrol so we had to go to the petrol station to get some. After that my friend said he wanted a new pair of swimming trunks so had to drive around until we found a shop that sold them. By the time we got to the swimming baths they were closed and we had to go back home. I was so depressed.

Maurice Moore

Dear Floella,

I suffer from spina bifida and have spent all my life in a wheelchair. I enjoy my life as my parents and friends have helped me to make my life a better one, and the quality of life I have received is good.

However, I do get annoyed and depressed at times. My disability I have accepted but I always get annoyed when people stare at me and talk above my head about me without talking to me. They never make any effort to talk to me or get to know more about me.

Nicola Cope

Chapter 12

How much am I worth?

LOTS OF PEOPLE SUFFER from low self-esteem, which means they don't like themselves. The strange thing about low self-esteem is that it's not something you are born with yet it can grow and stay with you all your life. It can take over your body and soul and rule your life. It can be destructive both for you and for anyone who comes into contact with you. What people with low self-esteem don't realize is that the reason they do bad things to themselves and others is because they hate themselves. The more bad things they do the worse it gets. People with low self-esteem sometimes put on a front so that they can face life. They act tough or dress aggressively or do outrageous things to hide their true characters. It's a shame they are prepared to do morally bad things in order to cope with the world. In many cases, if they were true to themselves they would have a great deal to offer.

Starting point

But how does this all start in the first place? Most people who do bad things usually say that it all started when they were children. As children some were made to feel unloved, some were abused. They were made to feel worthless and no good, which means someone was making them feel that way, it was not their fault. Once the feeling has got hold of them though it is very difficult to get rid of. They get the feeling that they can't do anything right. For others, parents' expectations can sometimes be too high and if they are not reached then a feeling of failure takes over. Some may not like the way they look and feel as if everyone is better looking than them. Some are constantly told that they are no good, and that they are clumsy and stupid by parents, teachers and peers. So they become trapped in a spiral of self-doubt and self-hatred. They forget how to love themselves and how to feel good inside.

Learning to love yourself

One of my favourite songs describes in detail how you should begin to love yourself. It's called "The Greatest Love of All". The words of this song ring in my ears every day and I try to pass on the message and the meaning of them not only to my children but to all the children I come into contact with.

The Greatest Love of All

I believe the children are the future,
Teach them well and let them lead the way.
Show them all the beauty they possess inside.
Give them a sense of pride, to make it easier,
Let the children's laughter remind us how we used to be.

Everybody's searching for a hero,
People need someone to look up to,
I never found anyone who fulfilled that need
A lonely place to be, so I learned to depend on me.

I decided long ago never to walk in anyone's shadow,
If I fall, if I succeed, least I lived as I believe,
No matter what they take from me, they can't take away
    my dignity.

Because the greatest love of all, is happening to me,
I found the greatest love of all inside of me.
The greatest love of all is easy to achieve,
Learning to love yourself is the greatest love of all.

And if by chance that special place,
That you've been dreaming of,
Leads you to a lonely place,
Find your strength in love.

Moral

What the song tells you is that learning to love yourself gives you dignity, makes you feel strong about yourself and as a result you refuse to do anything that will make you ashamed of yourself. If you can love yourself then it makes it much easier to love others and less easy to hurt them.

I'm bad and I know it

I know from talking to people who have done bad things that no matter how tough they make themselves out to be, how cool they are about being bad, how much they say they don't care about what they've done, deep down inside themselves they feel guilty and ashamed. It's only after talking with them in a very understanding way for a very long time that they will admit to these feelings. If you feel guilty and ashamed about yourself then you hate yourself and in turn you'll feel as if you want to hurt yourself. In some cases people take drugs which eventually kill them. Others turn to alcohol which also eventually destroys them, some don't eat. Some just become more and more violent and commit more and more crimes until eventually they are put into prison for a very long time. Some hurt the people they are supposed to love. It's all a way of confirming to themselves their belief that they are worthless human beings. They have been told they are bad over and over again until they believe it.

Mirror, mirror on the wall

How low is your self-esteem? When you look in the mirror, do you like what you see? For many people the answer is "No!" Of course most of us would like to change something about ourselves, straight hair for curly, blue eyes for brown, short for tall. We always seem to want the opposite to what we were born with, but all in all we learn to live with what we've got.

Unfortunately there are those who cannot accept themselves, they can't stand themselves at all. Many of these young people suffer from an illness called anorexia nervosa. Those who suffer from it believe that they are fat and ugly even though they are not. So they go on crazy diets to try and get slim. Eventually they give up eating altogether and starve themselves sometimes until they die.

Nowadays we are led to believe that everyone should be slim, beautiful and good-looking to be successful and happy. We see it all the time on television, in magazines and in films.

Young people are fed that message day in, day out. Even their peers go on about it when describing how they would like to look and no one ever wants to feel the odd one out. So some try to force their body to fit their mental picture of what they think is acceptable. That is when the trouble starts, they look in the mirror and in their minds they don't look like the images they see around them and the feeling of low self-esteem gets a grip on their very existence and starts ruining their lives.

Fitting into the mould

Before you try and squeeze into the mould ask yourself who is promoting the fact that you have to look a certain way in order to be beautiful, happy and successful? Is it those who are trying to sell their products and get rich out of you? Is it so-called friends who are only trying to put you down and aren't really friends at all? The answer is probably "yes" to both. If it is don't fall for it. Remember beauty is only skin deep, it's what you are inside that's important. Don't allow others to make you feel less about yourself. You were born the way you are and you should love yourself for the way you are. Always remember looks aren't everything.

When you love someone who is a beautiful human being inside, someone who is kind, thoughtful, considerate and caring but is not particularly good-looking, you realize that their looks are unimportant, it's what they are that's important. Good looks are only what we are brought up and led to believe are acceptable. I always say if you judge someone by their looks you will never know what you're missing out on. Someone could be good-looking, handsome or stunningly beautiful but they could be cruel and heartless with no thoughts or feelings for anyone but themselves – completely and utterly selfish. If you look around I'm sure you will see many people who don't fit into our society's ideal of beauty (they might be too skinny, too fat, too short or too tall) but they are nevertheless attractive because they have a certain style, flair and confidence in the way they carry themselves. Low self-esteem just doesn't figure in their thinking. They make the most of what they've been given, they don't try to hide the fact that they are not like everyone else. Neither do they make excuses about how they look, some even flaunt what they've been given in a positive way. If you feel that you aren't particularly good-looking you've just got to keep telling yourself that "it's not what you are on the outside that matters, it's what you are on the inside that's important." The more you feel that way the more people will feel that confidence radiating off you.

Are you on the danger list?

1. Do you feel ashamed of the way you look?

2. Are you embarrassed to speak out in public?

3. Do you wish you were someone else?

4 . Do you have a desire to inflict pain on yourself?

5. Do you think no one likes you?

6. Do you sometimes wish you were dead?

7   Do you want to make yourself look ugly?

8. Do you think everyone is better than you?

9. Are you afraid of being noticed?

10. Do you enjoy being told you are bad?

If your answers are "no" that doesn't make you conceited, it just means that you've got a healthy attitude towards yourself – keep it up! Mind you don't go over the top and think too highly of yourself, that too can be a symptom of low self-esteem .

However, if you answer "yes" to seven or more of these questions, then you are probably suffering from low self-esteem. It's not the end of the world, what you have to do is to start thinking positively about yourself.

Some days all your answers might be "yes". That's quite normal as long as the answers aren't "yes" the next day and the next and so on. If "yes" stays with you day in and day out, then it's time you did something about it.

Always look on the bright side

Now think about it carefully. I want you really to take a good look at yourself and write down all the things you like about yourself. Start with the smallest things. Like the fact that you don't bite your nails or you're good at skateboarding or you don't have smelly breath . This is the start of your foundation, the first building-block for your new image. Day by day you build up your foundation by adding new positive thoughts about yourself. If your peers try and put you down, turn it into a positive action by making a joke out of it. Think of it as them having a problem, not "you".

The next time you are about to do something to damage your new image, ask yourself, "Why am I doing this ?" If the answer is, "because I don't like myself", then force yourself to think about the things you like about yourself. All this won't come easy, you have to work at it but you'll be amazed at how quickly your self-esteem will grow. Keep telling yourself every day, "I am a worthwhile person," not in a boastful way but quietly and confidently .

Ten ways to boost your self-esteem

Only you can make up your mind to rebuild your self-esteem. It all starts with you not thinking everything is your fault and blaming yourself for things that go wrong. Don't keep apologizing for your existence and try to stop saying "sorry" for everything. You have to find yourself a workable plan and foundation to build on. Don't set your goals too high, just take one step at a time.

These are some suggestions as to how you can go about rebuilding your self-esteem.

1. Replace negative thoughts with positive ones.

2. Set new realistic challenges for yourself, small ones to start with so that you can reach them.

3. Have faith in your religion.

4. Refuse to let anyone put you down.

5. Practise smiling and getting on with others.

6. Look after your physical appearance.

7. Be kind and do good things for others

8. Don't give up on school, education is your passport to life.

9. Pick your friends with care.

10. Don't get disheartened if you are criticized. Take it on board, it could turn out to be useful.

Now you've got all the material to start building your self-esteem, it's not an impossible task, but neither is it easy. Build a little each day and you'll soon start to feel good about yourself. You'll be on the road to a new you, same face but with a different smile!

Dear Floella,
My baby sister is now four and because of her I keep being told off. I used to be really happy and like all the things I did but now I hate my life because everything I do is always wrong and everyone says how good she is. I always wanted a sister but now I wish I didn't.

Sam

Dear Floella,
I am not bad to look at but I have lots of
spots which are red. I do everything to
cover them up but nothing ever does. I
can never look at anyone and always keep
my eyes down. I know what everyone is
thinking. Whenever I hear anyone near me
laugh I feel as if they are laughing at me. It's
a horrible feeling I just wish my spots would
go away so I can feel good about myself.

Emily

Dear Floella,

I used to live with my grandmother, then one day my mother said she wanted me to come and live with her and her new family. I didn't want to go and my grandmother didn't want me to go either but my mother said I had to. I don't like living with my mother because we always argue. She says I am selfish and don't help enough. At school I haven't got any friends and no one likes me. They say I am too stuck up. I try to make friends but I can't. I used to be happy with my life and myself but now suddenly I am not.

Sonia

Chapter 13

What a wonderful world!

WHAT A WONDERFUL CREATION the planet earth is! All around us are natural wonders and beauty. No matter how technically advanced we become we will never be able to equal nature and create something as simple and breathtaking as a flower or a butterfly.

The human race takes its planet for granted and doesn't really look after it and care for it in the way it should. All the separate countries and groups who share the planet have to start thinking globally, in other words, it's no use throwing your rubbish over someone else's fence and thinking that's the end of it, it's their problem now. When a country dumps its pollution in the sea it washes up on another country's coast but it's still the same planet and eventually it will be everyone's problem. Nowadays we all know about the damage being done to the earth by pollution, so we really must get it into our heads that we are all responsible, every single one of us.

Nearly every day I see someone casually toss a piece of rubbish onto the ground. I've seen people throw glass bottles out of their cars onto the road, drop fast food containers on the street when they are standing only a few feet from a wastepaper bin. "What has this got to do with world pollution and the greenhouse effect?" I hear you say. Well it's got everything to do with it, because it's exactly the same attitude that causes people to dump nuclear waste into the sea, and cut down rain forests to make a quick buck. They think to themselves, "Well nobody's looking so I'll get away with it. Anyway what difference will a little bit of my nuclear waste make? It's only a little bit".

When I look around at some of our city streets I feel quite

sad to see them covered in filth, with litter and empty cans strewn everywhere. That is how the world is starting to look, because we all think our little bit won't make any difference. The truth is that we are all responsible, and your crisp packet does make a difference. I've often felt like putting on some rubber gloves and cleaning up the mess myself.

I'd like to get those who dump rubbish on the streets to be aware of their thoughtless acts because so many of them do it without thinking. We have all got to train ourselves to stop messing up the world and to keep it looking pleasant to the eye, because when your surroundings look good, you feel good too.

So the next time you feel the urge to chuck a piece of litter on the floor or smash a bus shelter or pull the branch off a tree or spray graffiti on a wall, think before you do it because your thoughtless actions are helping to mess up the world!

The lucky tree

There was once a king of Benares in India, who decided to build himself a luxurious palace. He told his builders that it must be supported by a great single column. The builders went out looking for a tree big enough to use. They found it in the Royal Park of Benares. It was the huge Sa-tree which rose majestically high above all the surrounding trees. The king told his builders to cut it down within seven days and use it to support his palace. But the men were afraid because it was a sacred and holy tree and they were sad for its spirit. They took flowers and gifts and laid them at the foot of the tree. They begged the tree-spirit to move away and live in another tree, but the tree-spirit could not live anywhere else and he told them he would die when the tree was cut down.

On the night before the tree was to be cut down the king was awakened by a light in his room. There in front of him was the tree-spirit dressed in splendid robes like a prince. "I am called the Lucky Tree, I bring happiness to everyone so why do you want to destroy me?" The king replied that he wanted the tree as the support for his new palace and that all who saw it would think he was a rich and powerful man.

"Very well", said the tree-spirit. "But when your men cut me down tell them first to cut off all my branches before they chop me down."

The king was shocked to hear that the tree-spirit desired such a slow, painful death. "Why are you asking this?" he asked the tree-spirit. "All around me are many young saplings, these are my children. If my tree with its spreading branches falls amongst them many of them will also die," replied the tree-spirit. "If I am to die at least my children will not be harmed."

At this the king felt ashamed. He realized that because of his vanity and selfishness he was prepared to destroy a thing of great beauty without thought.

The king looked at the tree-spirit and said, "Lord of the Forest, no harm will come to you or your children whilst I am king."

Moral

The moral of this story is clear. It's about the environment and the way we humans are destroying it for our own selfish and short-sighted needs. Needs which seem so important to us. But remember we are only on this planet for a very short time and if we carry on the way we are, we will destroy it for those who follow us.

We have to realize that, like the king in the story, our own selfish needs are far less important than the well-being of our planet.

Be part of your world

From a very early age children are keenly aware of the beauty of the world around them. They notice birds and the wonder of flight, they notice the different coloured flowers and the graceful movement of the fish. They are overawed by tiny insects as well as huge animals like whales, elephants and giraffes.

Unfortunately, somehow this sense of awe is eroded as they grow older. They become accustomed to living in a world where for the sake of progress and to make life more convenient for mankind, little interest is shown in preserving these wonderful creations. The world was created in a way that makes us all reliant on each other, trees, animals, birds, fish, insects and humans. In order for the world to survive as we know it, we have to take care of everything on our planet.

As a young person you are always being told that the world is in terrible danger. That if we don't watch out we are going to destroy it. It's all a bit depressing, especially if you are a child and love your world. After all, it's not you who invented all the cars and chemicals that are messing things up. You didn't make the generations before you do thoughtless things to spoil the environment.

At the moment you can't stop huge industries from pouring millions of tons of pollutants into the sea and the atmosphere for financial gain. They aren't going to listen to a few kids who ask them to stop, are they? So perhaps you may be discouraged from thinking about environmental problems and trying to do anything about them. It may seem like someone else's problem and you may feel you can do very little to make the world a better place. Forget that idea, you couldn't be more wrong. There are several ways that *you*, yes little old you, can make the world better.

1. Take care not to throw rubbish everywhere, put it in the right place.

2. Re-use and recycle everyday things and belongings.

3. Don't waste water, it's a valuable natural resource.

4. Save energy – turn off lights and turn down heating.

5. Start an environmental project at school, or with a group of friends.

6 Plant bulbs and seeds, even in a window box, because when the flowers come out they will make you aware of the beauty of your world.

7. Plant a sapling or a rose bush so that it will grow with you and will be there for your children and their children in the future. Remember trees are the lungs of the world.

8 Be aware of environmental issues and if you are angry about something write a letter to your MP either on your own or as part of your class.

9. Join an environmental group, so that you will get more information and be able to take a more active role in protecting the planet.

10. Don't be afraid to make adults aware that it's wrong when you see them doing environmentally unfriendly things.

We have been given a beautiful planet to live on and it's wrong to spoil it. When you grow up you will be far more aware of environmental issues than the people who are in charge now. So the future of the planet really does belong to you. I'm sure you will make a better job of it because from an early age you will have learnt what is right for your planet, for yourself, and for those who will follow you. Look after it, care for it and don't destroy it. Make the most of your world, it's the only one you've got!

Dear Floella,
I live in London and it is dirty and polluted.
Once I went to Wales with my school. It is
clean and the air is fresh to breathe there. I
wish everywhere in the world was like
Wales, especially where I live.

Tom Denton

Dear Floella,
My friends and I started a nature reserve on some waste ground near our school. We did a project on pollution and made an exhibition for parents' day. Everyone walked round the nature reserve and said it was very good.

I think everyone should look after their environment, because if we do not the earth will die.

Hillary Cowen

Chapter 14

The moment of truth

WELL, YOU'VE READ THE BOOK, now here's the quiz. The questions might reflect some situations that you have encountered at school or at home, on the sports field or in the street, with friends or foes. You may not have had the right answer or done the right thing when they happened to you. Hopefully now you've read this book you'll have the correct solutions.

See how you do. Just answer A, B or C to the following questions to see if you've understood the difference between right and wrong. Check your "Goodness Rating" at the end.

1. There is an old lady living near you. She cannot get out to the shops. Do you:
A. Throw stones through her windows.
B. Knock on her door and offer to do her shopping for her.
C. Just ignore her – she's just a silly old fool anyway!

2. You are bored and feel as if you haven't got anything to do. Do you:
A. Sit in your room feeling depressed.
B. Steal a car and go joy-riding with some other kids.
C. Do some work with a group raising money for charity.

3. A girl at school falls over and hurts her ankle. Do you:
A. Laugh at her and kick her bag so her books get blown all over the playground.
B. Help her to walk to a place where she can get help and rest her ankle.
C. Keep walking, saying she should be more careful.

4. **A classmate accidentally drops an expensive pair of trainers which he has saved up hard to buy. Do you:**
A. Hand them in to your teacher.
B. Leave them where they are and say "It's none of my business".
C. Pop them into your bag saying, "Finders keepers, losers weepers".

5. **Someone offers you something which you know to be stolen. Do you:**
A. Haggle to get the best price possible.
B. Tell him or her, "No thanks , you'd rather nick your own!"
C. Refuse to have anything to do with it and advise the thief to return it to its rightful owner.

6. **You see someone stealing something. Do you:**
A. Look the other way.
B. Say you want to split the profits or you'll tell.
C. Report what you've seen.

7. **You start at a new school and a few bullies gang up against you and demand money. Do you:**
A. Refuse to pay up and speak to someone about it.
B. Beat up someone younger than you and take their money.
C. Pay up to avoid getting a kicking.

8. **Everyone in the class seems to be picking on the same person every day. Do you:**
A. Join in as part of the gang to avoid getting picked on yourself.
B. Start an anti-bullying campaign in the school so everyone gets to know how to deal with bullying.
C. Make friends with the victim and stand up against the rest.

9. **Everywhere you go you seem to get picked on and teased. Do you:**

A. Wear a paper bag over your head.

B. With the help of an adult or friend try to find out what it is that makes people pick on you and if possible, do something about it.

C. Stop going out and stay away from school.

10. **Your best friend, for no reason, gets everyone in your class to turn against you and makes your life a misery. Do you:**

A. Pick a fight with your friend and try to force him or her to like you again.

B. Ignore him or her and find new friends.

C. Look at yourself in the mirror to see if there is something you are doing that you are not aware of.

11. **Someone steals your books so you can't revise for a test and you get low marks. Later on after the test the thief owns up and says it was a joke. Do you:**

A. Forgive them and say it was O.K.

B. Do the same to them.

C. Smack them around so they will never do it again.

12. **Someone who used to beat you up and bully you at your old school turns up at your new school and wants to be your friend. Do you:**

A. Have nothing to do with them.

B. Get your new friends to bully them and beat them up.

C. Say forgive and forget and become friends.

13. **You and someone at school are always fighting with each other. In fact you can't remember what started it. It's even affecting your school work. Do you:**
A. Walk up to your enemy and shake their hand and say, "Let's bury the hatchet."
B. Refuse to give in and keep up the battle.
C. Decide to finish it once and for all with a baseball bat.

14. **You are shy and wish you could join in with others who are having fun. Someone offers you something which they say will make you feel more confident. Do you:**
A. Say "Yes, but just this once".
B. Say no and walk away still feeling shy.
C. Tell them you'd rather be the way you are than rely on drugs to be brave.

15. **Someone tells you that you can earn loads of money by selling drugs for them. Do you:**
A. Report them to the nearest teacher, who will inform the head to have the kid expelled.
B. Do it for a short time until you earn the money you need.
C. Jump at the chance to make some easy money.

16. **You go to a party where everyone is drinking and taking drugs. Do you:**
A. Walk out at once saying, "This is not for me."
B. Pretend to join in so that no one will laugh at you.
C. Try to persuade your friends what they are doing is wrong.

17. **Your best friend gets a new computer as a surprise present. Do you:**
A. Nag your parents non-stop until they give you one even though they can't afford it.

B. Take one from someone who wants you to do something in return.

C. Be pleased for him or her.

18. The people who have all the latest gear, trainers, toys, sports equipment and stereos seem to be getting very popular and happy. Do you:

A. Spend ages wishing you were like them and forget everything else.

B. Be happy with what you have and tell yourself you are just as great as anyone else.

C. Hate your parents because they can't buy all the latest things for you.

19. Your parents are well off and you have everything. Do you:

A. Realize how lucky you are and try and give whatever you can to help others.

B. Feel superior and treat everyone else as peasants.

C. Show off all the time and boast about what you have got.

20. A new family has moved in next door to you. You want to be friends but your mates tell you not to. Do you:

A. Ignore your mates and do what you want to do.

B. Go along with your mates so that they stay your mates even though you know it's wrong.

C. Question if your mates really are your friends.

21. You find out that your best friend is of a different religion from you. Do you:

A. Exchange ideas about each other's religion.

B. Stop being friends.

C. Try to get your friend to change to your religion.

22. **You are from mixed race parents. Some people jeer at you and call you blackie, brownie and other racist names. Do you:**
A. Get into a big fight over it.
B. Say you're not.
C. Answer with pride, "I'm black and white which makes me golden and very special. What's so special about you?"

23. **You've just finished a bag of crisps and a can of drink on your way home from school. Do you:**
A. Toss it on the street, saying , "That's what road sweepers are for".
B. Wait until you find a bin to put it in or take it home with you.
C. Throw it over a fence into someone's garden, thinking now it's someone else's problem.

24. **You find a can of spray paint. Do you:**
A. Put it in the bin where it can do no harm.
B. Have a go at re-spraying your dad's car.
C. Write your name on the nearest blank wall you find.

25. **You see some mates playing in the park. They are swinging on the branches of a tree until they break off. Do you:**
A. Explain that trees take years to grow and are very important to the environment.
B. Join in and break a few more.
C. Build a bonfire with the branches and laugh as the smoke belches into the atmosphere causing more pollution.

26. On your way to school you see someone from a neighbouring school. They make a rude sign at you. **Do you:**
A. Pick up a nearby piece of wood and belt them over the head with it.
B. Smile to yourself and think what a sad case.
C. Get a group of mates together and head for the other school's gates to start a riot.

27. **You see a boy in school with a knife in his pocket. Do you:**
A. Get one for yourself so you can use it against him if he attacks you.
B. Join his gang so at least you are on his side.
C. Mention it to a grown-up who you can trust.

28. **Billy steals a charity box containing 75p from a shop. Who do you think will suffer:**
A. The charity and the people they are trying to help.
B. The shopkeeper.
C. No one, he didn't hurt anybody.

29. **Karen plays truant from school at least once a week. Do you think:**
A. She's having a good time.
B. Her education will suffer.
C. Her parents and teachers will be really upset to find out.

30. **A group of kids you know are doing a lot of house-breaking. Do you think:**
A. If they broke into your house and took your parents' video and your computer your family would be upset.
B. House-breaking must be brilliant and a really exciting way to get money.
C. Well, the people who own the house are rich and they are insured anyway.

31. **A girl at school has always carried a knife, one day she gets in a fight and stabs someone. Do you think:**
A. She'll be a heroine at school.
B. The girl will be arrested and put away.
C. The person she stabbed will not mind.

32. **You are supposed to be going to a party but on the day you are told you can't. Do you:**
A. Sit in your room and sulk, getting yourself more and more depressed.
B. Try and persuade your folks to let you go.
C. Get on with some things you have been longing to do.

33. **One of your friends has been getting depressed because she thinks she is fat. Do you:**
A. Try and convince her that she should be happy with the way she looks.
B. Agree with her and say you've noticed that she has been putting on a lot of weight recently.
C. Tell her you know of a good shop where they sell oversized clothes.

34. You are in your school cricket team, but lately your game has been getting worse and worse and you fear that your coach is going to boot you out of the 'A' team. Do you:

A. Resign before you are forced to.

B. Take some drugs and tell yourself they will make you a better player.

C. Practise in the nets for an extra two hours after you have finished your homework.

35. You want to join a drama club after school but you haven't got the confidence to apply because you think everyone is going to laugh at you. Do you:

A. Bottle out of joining at the last minute.

B. Tell yourself, "Everyone around me is human and has the same emotions as me."

C. Sit in the corner and tell yourself, " I can't do it ! " before you have even tried.

36. Susie has a birthmark on her forehead which looks like a terrible rash. She is always being teased and called moonface. If you were her would you:

A. Put loads of make-up on to hide your birthmark.

B. Reply calmly, "This is the way I was born and I still love myself, birthmark and all!"

C. Run and hide whenever you go out into the playground.

37. You are the best singer in your school choir and the music teacher asks you if you will sing a solo in the next singing competition. Do you:

A. Chicken out, saying you are not good enough to do a solo.

B. Jump at the opportunity of representing your school.

C. Agree to do it but don't turn up on the day.

38. If you saw someone being bullied. Would you:

A. Stand around and laugh.

B. Join in.

C. Try and defend them.

39. One of your mates needs money and he starts bullying to get it. Do you:

A. Tell him that is not the way to get it.

B. Help him bully to get the money.

C. If he doesn't listen to you, bully him and see how he likes it.

40. You are really unhappy because you are being bullied. Do you:

A. Cry and keep it to yourself.

B. Talk it over with your friends and family.

C. Start bullying someone.

Well how did you do? Did you come up with the right solutions to the dilemmas? Was it easy for you to work out what the right thing to do was and could you see clearly what was wrong? Check your goodness rating now. The answers are waiting for you.

Answers

1.	A= 0	B= 4	C= 2
2.	A= 2	B= 0	C= 4
3.	A= 0	B= 4	C= 2
4.	A= 4	B= 2	C= 0
5.	A= 0	B= 2	C= 4
6.	A= 2	B= 0	C= 4
7.	A= 4	B= 0	C= 0
8.	A= 0	B= 4	C= 2
9.	A= 2	B= 4	C= 0
10.	A= 0	B= 2	C= 4
11.	A= 4	B= 0	C= 0
12.	A= 2	B= 0	C= 4
13.	A= 4	B= 2	C= 0
14.	A= 0	B= 4	C= 4
15.	A= 4	B= 0	C= 0
16.	A= 4	B= 0	C= 2
17.	A= 0	B= 0	C= 4
18.	A= 0	B= 4	C= 0
19.	A= 4	B= 0	C= 0
20.	A= 2	B= 0	C= 4
21.	A= 4	B= 0	C= 2
22.	A= 0	B= 0	C= 4
23.	A= 0	B= 4	C= 0
24.	A= 4	B= 0	C= 0
25.	A= 4	B= 0	C= 0
26.	A= 0	B= 4	C= 0
27.	A= 0	B= 0	C= 4
28.	A= 4	B= 2	C= 0
29.	A= 0	B= 4	C= 4
30.	A= 4	B= 0	C= 0

31.	A= 0	B= 4	C= 0
32.	A= 0	B= 2	C= 4
33.	A= 4	B= 0	C= 2
34.	A= 0	B= 0	C= 4
35.	A= 0	B= 4	C= 0
36.	A= 2	B= 4	C= 0
37.	A= 0	B= 4	C= 0
38.	A= 0	B= 0	C= 4
39.	A= 4	B= 0	C= 0
40.	A= 0	B= 4	C= 0

Results

0-30 You need to rethink about yourself and others, about what's right and wrong, so read this book again, very carefully. You need help!

32-80 Not good enough, but you're on the right track, keep trying to do the right thing.

82-120 Excellent, you really do care about others and truly understand the difference between right and wrong.

122-160 Goodness me! you are a saint in the making. I only hope you didn't cheat!

Goodbye thought

I've enjoyed writing this book because it's made me think. I hope it's made you think a little too. You may feel that doing the things in this book will make you into a "square" or a "goody-goody" and make people laugh at you and call you names. But that's just it; everyone nowadays is afraid of speaking out and being good because of what others might say and do. That is why evil is winning and the world is in such a terrible state.

All I want you to do is to think about some of the things I've said and if you practise just a few of them it would be better than none. You will be doing what is morally right and only good can come out of that. Your efforts will benefit us all now, and future generations too. So remember to practise the three "Cs" which are **consideration**, **contentment** and **confidence**.

Best of luck. I'll be thinking of you whoever and wherever you are.